DEDICATION

To Rudy and Natalie, without whom there would be no book. It took "fire in the belly," and their flame burned brightly. Many dedicated people also believed in our dream and worked hard for it. They are mentioned in the book. To all the caring helpers and the world's children, there are not enough thanks to go around.

Char and Rudy in Glasgow

PAINTBRUSH DIPLOMACY

A Memoir

by Char Pribuss

Inquiries should be addressed to Paintbrush Diplomacy, Inc.
Find us on the World Wide Web at http://www.paintbrushdiplomacy.org

Bound and printed in the Unites States of America.

Book design by Barbara Lande.
Cover art by Char Pribuss.

ISBN 0-9717150-0-9

Library of Congress # 2001099366
First Edition

CONTENTS

INTRODUCTION

A magical combination of children, paint, brushes, and paper has produced a remarkable tale of an innovative diplomacy that has resulted in a greater understanding of other countries, other cultures. *Paintbrush Diplomacy*, an engrossing tale of two remarkable people, Char and Rudy Pribuss, will captivate the reader. You will be taken on a journey behind the Iron Curtain, to Checkpoint Charlie, and to more than 60 different countries. The precious art collected over a period of 29 years has been displayed at the United Nations, the Smithsonian Institution, and the San Francisco Airport.

It was our distinct pleasure to aid along the way by reaching out to diplomatic sources around the world.

Take a journey with *Paintbrush Diplomacy* and be reminded that the ingredients for peace are not only in the signature of a diplomat's pen but sometimes in the stroke of a child's paintbrush.

Congressman and Mrs. Tom Lantos
February 27, 2001

FOREWORD

By Laura Lemaire

What Is Paintbrush Diplomacy?

Paintbrush Diplomacy, a nonprofit organization, is an art and letter-writing exchange program for schools throughout the world. The founders of Paintbrush Diplomacy, my parents, Char and Rudy Pribuss from San Mateo, California, originally started the program in 1972. Traveling around the world, Char and Rudy brought the art of American students into foreign countries, often receiving art in exchange. In the talks they gave, Char and Rudy invited the students to continue exchanging their art and letters with that of children in the United States. The primary purpose of their travels was to foster the universal language of art.

Paintbrush Diplomacy became a nonprofit organization in 1986. Since that time, the program has evolved from a pen pal/art exchange program into an inter-disciplinary curriculum for schools, which has been enthusiastically utilized by teachers in all grade levels. Today, the objective of Paintbrush Diplomacy is to provide a worldwide communication and learning network based upon an annual theme. The program provides teachers and students with an opportunity to share ideas and to learn about each other. It emphasizes an interdisciplinary approach that combines social studies with other subjects such as writing, art, music, and science.

Paintbrush Diplomacy in the Classroom

Each school year, Paintbrush Diplomacy asks participating schools to address its annual theme. Themes from previous years include Geography, Myths and Fables, The Environment, The Global Family, Sports and Games Around the World, Inventors, Inventions and Imagination, and Foods of the World. These themes focus the program and provide a sense of world unity and commonality among students. Each participating class is matched with classrooms of similarly aged students from several foreign countries. Students are encouraged to study their exchange country and theme and to share writing and art that relate to the topic. The curriculum adapts well to brainstorming, group projects, and interdisciplinary working in a variety of subject areas.

Last year the annual theme was World Beat—Music from Your Country. As part of this project, the fourth grade students at Montclair Kimberley Academy in New Jersey decided to learn about songs that were part of American history and culture. The boys and girls studied such songs as "Yankee Doodle," "Swing Low, Sweet Chariot," "I've Been Working on the Railroad," "The Star-Spangled Banner," and "Take Me Out to the Ballgame." The students researched the historical context of each song, then wrote stories about what the song meant to them and to our country. Wonderful illustrations of the songs were included with the stories. Finally, each student wrote a letter about his or her self. They wrote about life in America, the things they liked in school, the games they played, the food they liked to eat. Photographs of the students were included in the package of materials that were sent to Paintbrush Diplomacy.

Later that spring, the Montclair Kimberley students received their exchange package from similarly aged students in Israel, Bahrain, Japan, Romania, Russia, and Argentina. Receiving the art and letters from these foreign students began several weeks of celebration, learning, and sharing. Groups of three students teamed together to learn about one of the assigned countries. Each team read the letters, went to the library for research, and knowing that we can learn much about a country from its artwork, studied the pictures for clues about the culture, dress, weather, and customs of the people. After gathering information, each team presented their findings to the class. Together, the class learned about the countries that had sent these wonderful diplomatic packages. It was an exciting project, and many students sent thank-you letters to the exchange countries.

Char and Rudy Pribuss' dream of communication and sharing among children of the world had come alive in this classroom—and in classrooms everywhere. The world is a little smaller because of the work started by my parents.

PREFACE

On a cold December day in 1978, I sat sketching the tiny fishing boats, bamboo shrubs, and tropical growth of Cheung Chau island, a short ferry ride from Hong Kong, as husband Rudy watched. Our government told us the People's Republic of China was off limits to U.S. citizens at that time, but we were adventurers who slipped through what was then known as the Bamboo Curtain via Canadian Airlines. Having been in China for three weeks, we were travel weary, and our bags were full of dirty laundry. But one last experience was impossible to resist.

Several little girls in red quilted jackets nestled at our feet, curious about what I was doing. Their bright colors and shining eyes moved Rudy to say, "No need for speech, art seems to be the international language."

Something indescribable passed between us. We were never the same two people again. Although we had started six years earlier to exchange the art and letters of U.S. children with that of children overseas, this moment was like an epiphany. We *knew* then that we were committed, deeply committed, to continue carrying the fruits of children's creativity and imagination around the world.

We visited 61 countries and stumbled on a grass-roots form of communication between the United States and young children of countries considered threats—countries against which our government imposed sanctions, countries with cultures most Americans didn't understand. Only the children could speak to each other through their creative gifts. We were the carriers. Our adventures brought Rudy and me together in a whole new way. Ours was a love story of two people making a tiny dent in a war-filled world of fear and distrust.

My engineer husband was born in Dresden, Germany, and raised with strict guidelines. He envied the other kids in their stylish dirty cords, while his were starched and pressed. The gypsy in him remained dormant until he married me, an artist.

Where was I before Paintbrush Diplomacy? San Francisco Art Institute, painting children's portraits for design-school tuition, art teacher, mother, and homemaker with hidden wanderlust. I was accustomed to taking chances. All this made Rudy and me a not-so-odd couple. We meshed. Trained as an engineer, Rudy solved the logistics of adventures that brought us from the streets of India to the jungles of Papua New Guinea to interrogation rooms in the Soviet Union. Once in 1984, at midnight and accompanied by rifle-carrying border police, we were thrown off a train crossing a Czechoslovakian forest.

How did two lone people get themselves into so many hair-raising situations?

Like Laurel and Hardy, or the drunk falling out of a building and remaining unharmed, innocence was often bliss. Once on a plane, we were transformed. Throughout our adventures, we held our portfolio of children's art and letters close to us, and they became our security blanket.

We saw TV aerials on tin shacks and mud huts from Rio to Jamaica to India, and knew life was no longer what it once was. Pandora's box was opened. Without diplomatic portfolio, we brought our combined gift to the ends of the earth.

After a night made sleepless by some travel-related illness in Darjeeling, I asked Rudy, "What do we think we're doing?" Neither of us had answers. We didn't think we were exactly changing the world.We hoped we were creating a small measure of understanding where there seemed to be none.

What one of us lacked, the other supplied. Rudy's engineering brains and slide rule kept us from falling off our path, and I was able to talk to any crowd on any stage like a wind-up toy, brimming over with zeal for our quest. Filling plastic hotel laundry bags to separate the art gifts was an inexpensive filing system. Our desire to keep going was fed by talking to "real" diplomats in our tiny bed-and-breakfast lodgings from Sweden to wherever. Getting close to a cigar-smoking, turbaned Indian Rotarian and mud-covered Papua New Guineans, and telling a little Swedish boy I would say hello to John Wayne for him (although John Wayne had been dead about four years), offered rewards we could never explain. Many thought we had dinner with movie stars each night because we lived in San Francisco. Such things fired our unquenchable spirit. Lost luggage did not worry us, although precious contacts were sometimes in it. Other contacts continued to arrive.

Once a year for three weeks our four children were watched over by generously caring grandparents, Oma and Opa. The children prayed for our safe return and the eldest, when picking us up at San Francisco International Airport, looked at Rudy's China-grown beard and said to his brother, John, "Where did we go wrong?"

How did a program known as Paintbrush Diplomacy start? How could it cover the world by the year 2000? Probably by accident.

From the children who gathered at our feet on Cheung Chau island to the classrooms of Saudi Arabia, we often felt pulled along by more than our own efforts. Bringing a handful of U.S. children's art gifts to China in 1978 was our first ticket into a regime closed to Americans. Only when the children's art from around the world started pouring in, and we were housing it in our bathtub and bagging it in packs under our beds, did we realize we had a tiger by the tail, and a bankbook that couldn't contain it. Our project had become a success bigger than two people could deal with. In 1986, out of necessity, we made Paintbrush Diplomacy a non-profit organization. Our "mom and pop"-type operation became more businesslike. A director, Germaine Juneau, came to us from the Smithsonian Institution. She and our board of directors helped our dream continue.

What do we expect for the future as a result of our international exchange of children's art? We can't guarantee that a tin-wrapped painting from a student in

Iraq, showing enemy bombs falling on his city, will change the outlook of a San Francisco student. We can guarantee that with children's art, we've brought the best of the United States to a welcoming world.

A lot of love paved a sometimes bumpy road for Rudy and me. Basically we weren't worried about looking like travel clothing advertisements. When on unheated trains, I tied wool socks around Rudy's bald head. He wrapped his wool muffler around my hands and we bundled. Hollywood love scenes don't compare.

I have written about some of our more bungee jumping kind of experiences and have included art (kids' and mine). Grandparents can still bounce around! Ask our ten grandchildren.

Now retired, the engineer is still on the board of Paintbrush Diplomacy. Although Parkinson's disease has slowed him down, he does everything but steal to keep their revenue coming. We hope our children, their children, and the world's children will remember what these paintbrush diplomats did and will pick up their own "paintbrush" to create a brighter world. We say, "Good luck, and go for a masterpiece!"

Char Pribuss
June 1, 1997

[Editor's Note: While Char and Rudy's *Paintbrush Diplomacy* story was written during his lifetime, Rudy died in December 1997. He left knowing that the Char and Rudy Pribuss International Children's Art Museum for Paintbrush Diplomacy was located in the historic World Trade Center (the Ferry Building) amid the shipping piers of San Francisco Bay.]

THE BIG DREAM

United Nations—1988

Rudy and Char at the U.N.

Looking out the window of the main plaza in the United Nations building this day in April 1988, I feel like a sleepwalker moving back into another era of my life. On the floor lies a large collection of international children's art my husband, Rudy, and I have been asked to mount for an exhibit. Paintbrush Diplomacy, a program we founded in 1972, has made it to the Big Apple!

My thoughts drift back to my first experience in the United Nations with our own four grade-school children in 1968. We had decided to cross our country on a shoestring, looking like something out of *The Grapes of Wrath*—suitcases rope-tied to the top of our temperamental station wagon. We slipped children through windows of motel rooms not meant for six and made lunch on our beds to pack in a leaky freezer chest for the next day's journey. Bedraggled as we looked, Rudy suggested we start with the U.N. building.

We felt transformed when we walked along the International Plaza to the entrance of this multicultural gathering place. We tried to explain to the children its purposes. A young Indian guide showed us meeting rooms where no gains might have been made that day but where hope could still grow the next. We discussed the difficulty of so many people of different cultures trying to build an understanding with each other in order to bring about a more peaceful world.

"Well," said daughter Laura, "if all the people of the world talk friendly to each other, there won't be war anymore, will there?"

"Maybe yes, maybe no," said Rudy, "but if a small war is stopped because of a friendly talk where people learned something about each other, isn't that still worth it?" We could see that she expected a more positive answer.

"Settling for even the smallest bit of good is always better than nothing," I offered.

Twenty years later I sifted through our collection of children's art that Rudy and I had been given in countries all over the world. Paintbrush Diplomacy had taken on a life of its own. Sometimes I wonder how—perhaps because Rudy and I had worked hard over the years, going to every school where we were asked to speak, bringing our art and letters from the United States.

Our mission brought us from India to Appalachia, from America to China (even before our country's normalization of relations with that country). We sought out schools in remote areas of the world. Never leaving home without our students' art gifts and letters, we often looked like door-to-door peddlers with our frayed art portfolio.

Sometimes we even wore backpacks filled with children's T-shirts picked up at our Goodwill stores. We packed crayons, paint boxes, erasers shaped like the Statue of Liberty. Once we even brought Michael Jackson pins into the Soviet Union—as coveted as Oscar awards by aspiring thespians! Especially in smaller countries we visited, everything we brought—from U.S. student art to gifts of all kinds—was received with overwhelming joy.

Remembering our Laura's question many years ago, she could now ask, "Have you and Dad stopped a war by bringing young people's art and letters for exchange around the world? Will children in these countries' schools grow into more peace-loving adults because of your efforts?"

My answer: "We'll never be sure."

What we do know is that many classrooms in the United States are now connected with foreign classrooms, writing letters and sending art because of our little "mom and pop" idea. Other travelers pack suitcases with a lot less unnecessary clothing and more U.S. children's paintings. They return with foreign children's art gifts.

We don't have our own gallery, but until this dream can come true, Rudy and I are down on our knees in the U.N. building, sorting our treasures for their gallery space. Eight hours of this kind of work brings sore feet and stiff legs. Opening day we forget our aching bodies.

The Honorable Herbert S. Okun, permanent representative of the United States to the United Nations in New York City, introduces us with kind words for our endeavors, matched by enthusiastic support from Joseph V. Reed, undersecretary general for political and General Assembly affairs, and Mrs. Anne Murphy, wife of Richard W. Murphy, assistant secretary of state for Near Eastern and South Asian affairs. A young people's symphony group from London plays. Spotlights shine on the children's art, making the display even more striking. We burst with pride, feeling that the young artists who gave us their art are our own!

In 1986, we had mixed feelings when—through necessity—our program became a nonprofit corporation. Sometimes Rudy and I patted each other on the back with tears in our eyes. Actually, the two of us could no longer talk in schools throughout the world, mat art, collect U.S. art, hang shows, do interviews, kiss our newborn grandchildren, and retain our sanity. Friends from our local art council offered to help us by forming a nonprofit corporation.

Overnight my art studio became an office. The Rotary Club kindly lent us a

Aborigines Age 10

Aborigines Age 10

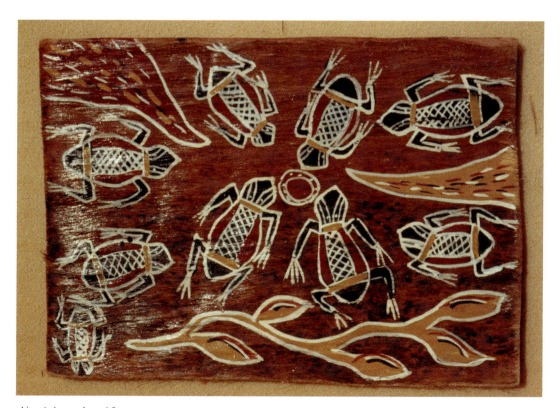

Aborigines Age 10

Aborigines Age 10

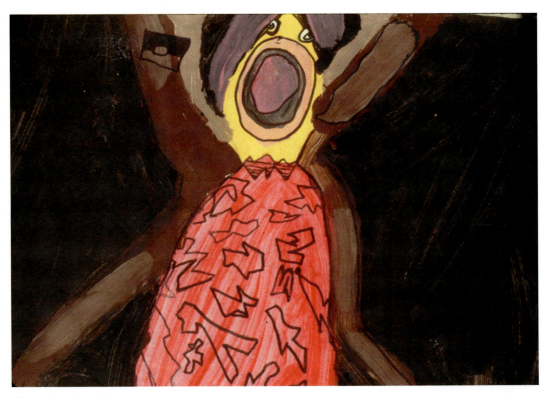

Aborigines Age 10

Aborigines Age 11

Argentina Age 13

Argentina Age 13

Argentina Age 17

Argentina Age 14

Argentina Age 14

Argentina Age 16

Australia Age 10

Australia Age 11

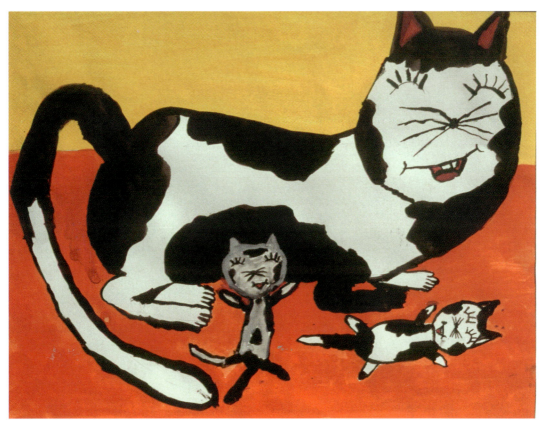

Bahrain Age 9

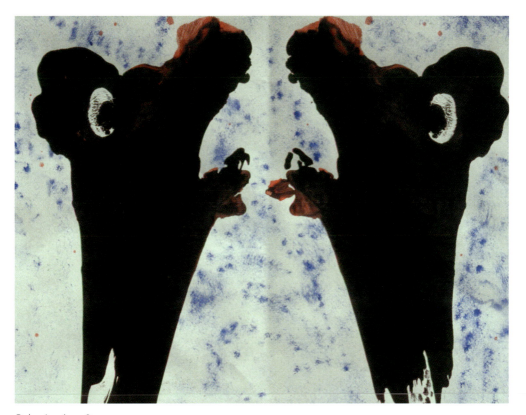

Bahrain Age 9

Bahrain Age 12

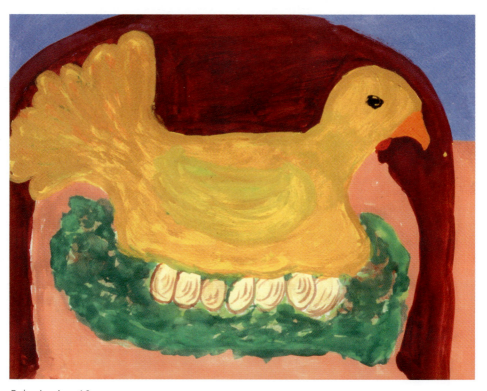

Bahrain Age 10

Bahrain Age 7

Bahrain Age 11

Bahrain Age 11

Bahrain Age 12

Bahrain Age 11

Bahrain Age 12

Bahrain Age 12

Bahrain Age 11

Bhutan Age 5

Bhutan Age 5

Bhutan Age 12

Bhutan Age 12

Bolivia Age 10

Brazil Age 10

Brazil Age 10

Brazil Age 13

Canada Age 13

Canada Age 11

computer, a parade of volunteers, and a paid executive director. People came and went from our home like a stream of ants. I withdrew to a corner of my dining room with my old manual typewriter and attempted to write this book about our 14 years of travel with Paintbrush Diplomacy. Nobody told me how an artist writes a book!

Two years later, in 1988, the program occupied a section of a local high school. Art that had been "filed" in our bathtub was now kept in a beautiful, donated cabinet. Volunteers and our executive director moved more comfortably. I had my art studio back. Sales of my own art went to feed the children's program. Rudy and I spent a good deal of our time in the fund-raising business—a new experience this! The program was solvent and we never looked back, even when it seemed the sheriff was one step behind us. Today people want to join the program through schools, travel agencies, humanitarian and other organizations.

We couldn't believe our good luck, but we often cried "Help!" The bigger the program grows, the more volunteers we need, and the more funding we must have. With the help of the Chevron Corporation, we had our own videocassette, made partly in a Leningrad school and partly in a U.S. classroom. It explained the program fully and was accompanied by a guideline packet and membership information.

The time had now come for us to leave our dream show at the United Nations. The TV cameras have recorded it all, so we have evidence of the program's reality. Our swollen feet and lack of sleep seem to have vanished, and we still retain the feeling of joy that we think permeated the U.N. building. Many notes written in our U.N. guest book have left heartwarming offers. We hope that some will be our life preservers when we feel stretched too thin. Packing up our world-traveled and frayed art portfolio, we wave goodbye to the U.N. security guard as he locks up this building for another night.

Entering the darkening streets of New York, Rudy and I wonder where our hopes will bring us next. As the fast-moving traffic skims past us, I answer little Laura's question one more time. "Yes, Laura, it's all been worth it. Dreams do matter."

THE POLISH TRAIN

Krakow to Prague—1971

Krakow, Poland

We had the option of getting a train from Krakow to the nearby town and waiting in the train station for two hours for the connecting train, or paying $50 for a cab ride and catching the train with only half an hour wait. The $50 started sounding more and more like a bargain. A driver arrived out of the cold rain, and Rudy and I settled in the back seat hoping to get a couple of good hours of sleep.

The friendly Polish people could not do enough for us—our driver was no exception. A few minutes of quiet were interrupted by the sound of his car heater rattling like an ancient coffee grinder. Car heaters always brought me back to days of my pregnancies and instant nausea.

I took off my many layers of wool clothing, breathed deeply, and decided to accept his warm hospitality like a good sport. Still he could not do enough. Lulled into a half-sleep by the heat of the car, I was awakened by loud American rock music interspersed with what seemed like ethnic Polish folksongs. Looking into the driver's rear view mirror, I saw a gracious smile from our driver. He knew he had hit a chord!

Finally arriving at the train station at midnight, we felt the hard part was over and we could coast in. Little did I know the real test had just begun for us.

We sat in the cold depot, body to body with Polish people. An old woman had rags wrapped around her legs. We traded body heat. A slightly drunken man passed, eyeing our luggage. It was not that luxurious, but I was almost ashamed to have it.

Once on the train, we discovered our first-class compartment in no way resembled those inhabited by movie stars embarking on romantic adventures. To say it was similar in size to a fair-sized closet would be more than generous. Putting two suitcases in an overhead rack and adjusting our bodies to this tiny space was quite a feat; we both sat on the small lower berth, panting. Getting six-foot Rudy up the tiny ladder and into the upper bunk proved impossible.

When a toothless "train handyman" appeared and took control, we were glad to move into the aisle and give him the keys to our compartment. He put sheets on our tiny beds and adjusted leather straps to keep Rudy from falling out of bed. A couple of U.S. dollars brought about his sweetest smile yet.

Now to sleep. Even with an ancient train fighting old, uneven tracks, I dozed off for about a half-hour but was brought to complete consciousness by the pounding of a military policeman's club on our door. He carefully scrutinized our passports and, starting from the first page, repeated the process several times. Our photos couldn't have resembled the wild, disheveled faces he observed. After what seemed like a lifetime, he handed our papers to me and departed. A half-hour later, either dozing off or unconscious, I heard another demanding club on my door. A second military police officer entered.

"What now?" Rudy complained.

"Don't rock the train," I called up to him. Banging the sections under my bunk, around our luggage, and above Rudy's head, he then explored all areas not taken up by our bodies or luggage and departed.

"I think he was looking for a hidden body," Rudy laughed.

We finally arrived at the Prague depot hours later with three questionable hours of sleep, dragging our luggage for what seemed like miles. As we waited for a cab, we looked at each other. I realized these are the times when beauty and romance have nothing to do with a lasting marriage.

A bath and a decent hotel room can do wonders for the human spirit. Eight hours of sleep can do more, but I will never forget any of the Polish train experience. Mostly I will never forget two Americans from California grateful for the warmth of poor Polish bodies huddled next to ours in a cold depot one cold midnight.

USSR—ROUND ONE

Yerevan, Armenia—1976

Uzbekistan

Chaz

We had heard much about a children's museum in Yerevan, Armenia. Like two hunting dogs, we immediately pointed in its direction.

We discovered it's difficult to leave a tour group and go off on one's own, but Paintbrush Diplomacy becomes more important to us than any tour guide's description of a cathedral or items of interest on a city tour. Sometimes rejoining a group after once leaving it can lead to trouble. For example, in India we left the tour to visit a school in New Delhi and almost lost the group—and did lose all of Rudy's luggage. We found the group but never the luggage.

Taking our chances, we left the group in Yerevan for the children's gallery. After two tries, we arrived five minutes before closing. When the door shut and locked behind us, Rudy and I were the sole viewers of the children's art. A little intimidating in a communist country, but a soft voice behind us soon alleviated our uneasiness.

"I heard your comments to your husband," she smiled. "You must be an artist."

"Art, the universal language, has done it again," I remarked.

After I gave an enthusiastic American art teacher's response to each painting and piece of sculpture, the gallery attendant and I became a mutual admiration society. Rudy explained our program, and before we knew it, she led us down a long, dark corridor to meet the gallery director on another floor. The old cliché, "What's a nice suburban American couple like us doing in a place like this?" flashed through my mind. As we finally entered an office lined with posters of children's art from around the world, we knew why we had persevered.

We mentioned that San Francisco is our home base. The director, who looked like my sweet elderly aunt, responded, "Do you go to the San Francisco concerts of Seiji Ozawa?" A Japanese-American symphony conductor and children's art made two Armenians and two U.S. travelers seem like old friends. This only reinforced our belief in the productive bonding children and art can bring.

The Armenian director explained how their exchange program worked. All their art was sent to participating countries "for keeps." Postage and the undependability of the mail systems, plus out-of-reach expenses for some, made returning art too difficult. We discussed the possibility of an exchange show between our coastal California children and the children of Yerevan. All looked so simple—we began wondering why our governments were in conflict when the four of us were so compatible.

The remainder of our trip flowed through Southern Russia into the Muslim cultures of Uzbekistan, Samarkand, Tashkent, and Bukhara. The beautiful mosque tiles depicting patterns of nature, the veiled ladies, and the haunting prayer chants will always be with me. A woven wall hanging I purchased will continue to spice up my dinner parties, but nothing stands out as much as our meeting in the basement of Yerevan's children's art museum.

Once home, we received a message saying that children's art from Yerevan was on the way. We built our life around its reception. Should we clear a space in the garage, moving my art into the rafters? Should we take time off before its arrival? Who would be here to receive it? Such needless anxiety—the art never came.

How many lessons we have learned of the workings of governments. You would think dealing with such an innocent commodity as children's art would make such lessons unnecessary. Several years after the Armenian encounter, the Russian ambassador in Washington told us that our President Carter's "unacceptable" human rights program would have caused our lost contact with Yerevan.

Rudy believes that nothing is difficult. Told that a task is impossible, he believes that it may just take a little longer to accomplish. We are a good team—adventuresome, caring, and probably indefatigable, so we keep moving.

BREAKING THE LANGUAGE BARRIER

China—1978

Shanghai, China

For 20 American people, arriving at the airport in Beijing in 1978 was like landing on Mars. We came by Canadian Airlines because our government does not have "normalization" with China. U.S. commercial flights bypass that country. Adventuresome, well traveled, we could hardly wait to enter the People's Republic of China.

Lawyers, artists, engineers, doctors, weavers, and the just plain curious made up our group. We looked at each other in a half-darkened Chinese waiting room while Mao-clad workers looked at us as curiosities. For 30 years they had observed few of our blue eyes, not heard our unbridled laughter, or seen clothes like ours.

An American woman in purple tights, fur jacket and hood was a show-stopper. I boasted the American skin-covering blue jeans. Husband Rudy sported his World War II overcoat. "It isn't stylish," I admonished, but December in China made me envy him. I had only my short, shabby, moth-eaten fur jacket, last worn with a rubber dog mask by our young daughter for Halloween. "The mask might have helped my cold cheeks," I whispered.

Many of the group sought knowledge from barefoot Chinese doctors, weavers, and painters. Rudy and I grasped a handful of U.S. children's paintings to give to Chinese children with the hope of their returning art to our kids—our "mom and pop" communication dream, Paintbrush Diplomacy. As an artist, I sketched wherever we traveled, discovering, as people often gathered around me, that language was not necessary. We seemed to join without trading a word. "Art looks like the universal language," observed Rudy, watching children gather at my feet as I sketched.

None of our group had met before, but we had one thing in common as we waited at our cold first stop. We were restless Americans, not good at waiting. There were few planes besides ours, the landing field was sparsely lighted, and an eerie feeling enveloped us as we staggered into the darkness. Had time stopped for these people? Were we prepared to bridge the gap of 30 years?

Our hospitable Chinese guides had a packed schedule for us. Rudy's and my first stop was a phone booth, hoping to contact an American government representative.

"Don't forget," I reminded Rudy, "we don't have normal relations with these people." Comical, because we get along famously with everyone from cooks to guides. Huddled together in the phone booth to keep from freezing in spite of our layering, we made a surprisingly quick connection with our man in Beijing.

"Well, no, Mr. Pribuss," the American voice returned, "I did not receive any information you mention sending to the U.S. State Department. From your explanation of the children's program, I would say you are a couple of years too early. Right now the Chinese are interested only in mechanical technology and sophisticated business methods. I will, however, drop your name at social gatherings."

Lifting my earflap, Rudy relayed his message, "Shall we go it alone?"

"I'm game," I shivered, my hands in the pockets of his World War II overcoat, which began to look more and more like a designer's masterpiece. Like a St. Bernard, Rudy produced a small brandy flask from his backpack. We shared a warm healthy swallow—for medicinal purposes, of course.

Our wonderful young Canadian guide supplied just what we needed. She worked behind the scenes with the Chinese guides, in an effort to promote our children's exchange. Her constant reminder: "Don't give up on the first try; they're *thinking.*"

The next featured event was a train ride to the Great Wall. "Wear everything you brought," we were told. "This will be the coldest time most of you have known."

Emptying my suitcase, I started with flannel pajamas, adding everything— ending with my fur jacket. If the jacket had been black and white instead of brown, I could have been taken for a well-fed panda.

Assigned various compartments, each looking like an intimate little sitting room with white doilies on chair arms and headrests for each seat, we were four passengers with a small teak table holding a beautiful dwarf tree and Mandarin oranges on an embroidered doily as a center piece. Somehow separated from Rudy, I ended up with two Mao-clad tour conductors—Mr. Woo and Mr. Yee.

Riding backward, as the wheels of the train clanged along, I faced two inscrutable-looking Chinese gentlemen. I couldn't avoid their stoic gaze. Suddenly, I was pulled from my lethargy by the older guide. "Why did you want to come to my country?" he asked.

"I can't talk about all I would like to bring to your country," I stammered, "because I was briefed before leaving the States on what topics to stay away from."

We laughed. He showed a smile nearly closing his eyes. I felt as though I were peeking through the Bamboo Curtain.

"You can talk to me about anything you want."

We discussed countries my husband and I had visited. He was hungry for my views on the different countries, but I tried to remain neutral on any political issues. When the train stopped, I was sorry we had had so little time together. All conversation took place between Mr. Woo and me. Mr. Yee, the younger man, only listened. I was about to rejoin the group when I realized the young guide stood alone and had something to say to me.

"Pardon," he asked shyly, "I would like a very big kindness from you. Could I have a few minutes?"

"Of course," I said, totally taken by surprise, as I had not heard anything voiced by Mr. Yee until now. He told me he was a teacher of English, at a boys' school.

Apologizing for his command of English, he asked, "Do you think you could give me a few American slangs?"

Having four children, I had a wealth of what he wanted.

This may be a whole new form of East-West diplomacy. For starters: "That's how the cookie crumbles," I offered.

"Ah, translation, please." He wrote enthusiastically with notebook in hand. Translating American slang is not the easiest task in the world. I gave him the best smile I could come up with before the group left me behind.

"That's fate," I suggested. Thereafter, Mr. Yee awaited me after each stop.

"Big shot": I walked around with thumbs in an imaginary vest, puffing on an imaginary cigar. "Ah," he smiled. "Person thinking he is too important."

"Cool cat": What to say? "Person admired by the young and impressionable," I explained. Mr. Yee's sincerity and dedication had me feeling a little guilty, but his joy drove me on until a yellow flag from our leader directed the group forward.

"Laid back": Hard for the communist-trained, industrious Mr. Yee to grasp, but he seemed to delight in its concept.

Before we were through, Mr. Yee had a book full of "slangs." We missed only one day of our linguistic camaraderie. Asked where he'd been one day when he hadn't appeared, he said with a mischievous smile, "I had other fish to fry." We had become players in a game.

Two days after our train ride, an older Chinese guide approached us, explaining he would like our presence the next day at a school auditorium where their children had something for us. Our Canadian guide felt we might be on the right track and promised to get us there.

The next day, we were taken to what was called the art room. Children sat at long tables doing paint-by-number portraits of Chairman Mao. As an abstract artist, I was in shock—I had hoped to see Chinese children's expressions of creativity. I hid my disappointment with difficulty.

Never down for long, we looked forward to our upcoming outing in a large, cold auditorium. We sat bundled up. Refills of delicious, very welcome hot tea came our way. A Chinese teacher and two tiny Chinese girls appeared on stage. Although the name called out seemed foreign to us, we finally realized, with some nudging from our guide, that we were to go on stage. Handed three tiny ribbon-tied scrolls, we were thanked for 12 pieces of U.S. children's art slipped to them by

Barbara Shannon, our loyal guide, who was becoming the third member of our team. We bowed and thanked them profusely.

Returning to our seats, Rudy muttered "What are we going to give the other nine U.S. kids when we come home with three Chinese children's paintings?"

"Shush, don't look a gift horse in the mouth."

Back in our hotel room, which resembled a film setting from *Ninotchka* with Greta Garbo, we sat on our tiny beds and untied the scrolls. Thirty beautiful brush paintings floated to the floor. On thin rice paper, they portrayed, with elegance and grace, cherry blossoms and scenes of intricately decorated pagodas set in manicured gardens. At our feet we carefully placed together the paintings, which now resembled a beautiful hand-woven rug. We looked at each other and cried. Previously tired, cold, and beginning to doubt our efforts, tears of joy flowed easily. These pure gifts have no expectation of return. Distanced by layered clothing, we embraced—words unnecessary.

Before leaving China, we visited communes. We applauded remarkable acrobats and watched barefoot doctors work in their makeshift clinics. One doctor had acupuncture needles placed in a patient's head.

"What does he suffer from?"

When he responded, "hypertension," I wondered how a worker in the rice paddies, surrounded by nature, could have one of our Western culture's ailments. I only nodded.

While our eyes were fascinated, privileged to see what Americans had been cut off from for many years, our greatest thrill was the Chinese children's art.

"What can we do for our wonderful Chinese guides?" We were told in no uncertain terms that true communists did not accept what Americans referred to as tips. Blue jeans! I tied the legs of mine around my fur jacket, which Mr. Yee admired, threw it under the bed, and pinned a note on top: "Fair exchange is no bad bargain. Love to all, Char and Rudy Pribuss."

"ADIÓS, CARLOTTA Y RODOLFO!"

Guadalajara, Mexico—1979

Girl in Mexico

When we go on a "short trip" it usually starts out something like this: "Let's not bring any children's art. This time we'll just get a good rest. Right, Char?"

"Sounds good to me," I say, knowing how much my battered body could use a total pass-out, lie-in-the-sun rejuvenation. Somehow, a few paintings always manage to find their way into the bottom of the suitcase. Inevitably they wind up winking at me.

On this trip, we met our friends, the Boleks, who had been living in Guadalajara, Jalisco. Sally, an artist friend in the States, was fascinated with our children's art and letter exchanges. Let's face it, Paintbrush Diplomacy is as much a travel necessity as credit cards, underwear, and "turista" medicine.

In Guadalajara, getting our bearings before meeting with Sally and Frank, we strolled around our hotel area when I noticed a pair of beautiful iron gates leading to what appeared to be a religious gift shop.

"Let's take a look in here. Maybe we can buy your mother a candle or something."

As we passed through the gates, a bell rang. From everywhere children converged on us. It appeared we were drawn, as though by a magnet, into a Mexican schoolyard.

"Let's face it," Rudy laughed as a little Mexican boy threw a ball near us. "It's in our court and we know we're going to run with it."

Through sign language and my broken college Spanish, we wove our way through a network of exhilarated Mexican children. The word "principal" sounds pretty much the same in Spanish and English. Before long little María led us to the principal's office.

How patiently he listened as we tried to explain Paintbrush Diplomacy! Señor José, understood a great deal more English than he spoke. We traded a little

English, a little fractured Spanish, and a great deal of hand language from Rudy. Sometimes hand language is the most successful of the three. We arranged to return with our student art the next day, and the following day we would pick up that of the Mexican children. At least I *thought* that was what we had decided upon.

After separating the art for Sally and Frank from that for our new school friends, we were off to School Urbana 63 the next day, to the sound of crowing roosters, barking dogs, and church bells—felt pens, Mexican candy, and my trusty Spanish dictionary in hand.

"If we only leave our art gift and the candy, it's still better than if we hadn't made the move."

"Right, even this much has been fun."

With a slight refresher course in Spanish the night before, I felt somewhat more confident when meeting the principal again. Had we expressed well enough our desire to carry his students' art and letters back to our classrooms? We could only hope for the best.

The school seemed quite poor. In spite of his responses of "sí, sí" and "perfec-tamente," we hoped we had not asked for what may have been impossible. Too often we Americans think all kids have art supplies and school pictures. We have learned this isn't true.

Entering the school, we immediately noticed a different atmosphere. No children were in evidence. All was very quiet. Señor José sat in his office dressed in Sunday best. Rudy and I in our California casuals felt a little understated. We were ushered into an area—part classroom, part patio—to find the entire student body seated, dressed in their best, hair slicked down or ribboned, anxiously waiting. We noticed parents and teachers. We were undone.

"There's more," Rudy whispered. "Look at the art on the walls." Carefully mounted American children's art of Snoopy, Superman, Mickey and Minnie Mouse, and all else the world's children love, accompanied paintings depicting typical American life. The audience oohed and ahed. The opposite side was adorned with nicely mounted Mexican children's art. On the bottom of each painting or drawing was a small school photo of José Gonzales, María Lopez, Roberto Santos, to name a few. "These are for you," the principal pointed to his children's art.

"Gracias, gracias," hardly seemed an adequate response. I checked the dictionary —"Espléndido, excelente!" We wanted to hug everyone, but this appeared to be just the beginning. Apparently there was an upcoming program—and we were it! An antiquated microphone and translator were brought forth. We were on.

We have given "presentations" all over the world. Often to our surprise, with no forewarning, we have found ourselves on a stage, surrounded by potted palms. We know how it feels to be a stand-up comedian. If you don't step lively, you're apt to lose your audience—especially restless children who have to wade through an interpreter to get the message.

At the end of the presentation, treats for all included a little cup of ice cream and a cookie. The principal gave each teacher the candy bags we brought to distribute as they chose, along with the felt pens. But the U.S. children's art was obviously the winner.

As we left our school, children followed in single file down the street, waving and calling, "Adiós, Carlotta y Rodolfo." When we entered the lobby of our hotel, this caused quite a show for the tourists.

"Just a little time and love," we informed an American woman who asked our secret. She now has our flyer on how she, too, can evoke in little ones a desire to follow her own "yellow brick road."

What about our friends, Sally and Frank? We arrived at their home in good condition, but with a little heavier luggage, thanks to our Mexican children's art gifts. They were amazed to hear our story. After living in Mexico for several years, they found our quick exchange surprising.

"*Mañana* is the password here," Sally explained. "Frank and I have adopted a slower pace, too." She worked with children in an orphanage and was very interested when we brought her up to date on Paintbrush Diplomacy. We departed, with Sally offering to send more art from Jalisco. We offered more from U. S. schools.

Once again on our own, Rudy and I, as usual, had to agree that the highlight of our Mexican adventure was the memory of the Mexican children, in single file, following us to our hotel with their shouts of "Adiós, Carlotta y Rodolfo!" Their art has been shared in many of our schools, civic centers, the San Francisco City Hall, and cultural centers everywhere. How little could we have known, walking through that iron gate, how much would open to their children and ours.

"Gracias, niños!"

THIRST QUENCHER

Jamaica—1980

Jamaica

Like many other people who now travel with our art and notes from the United States, our friends Ann and Arnold Anderson brought student art from their local grade school in Castro Valley, California, to Italy and Jamaica. Returning with art from those trips brought added flavor to their vacation.

"Like you guys, Char," Ann told me, "Arnold and I are now Paintbrush Diplomacy addicts." She turned over her contact in Blue Fields, Jamaica. "Virus awaits you with open arms." Fortunately, Virus was the teacher's name, not the bug we can do without!

Throwing together the minimum clothing and a pack of U.S. student art in a suitcase, we were off to Jamaica. Thanks again to the Andersons, our housing would be in a semi-guesthouse, as our hotel plan had fallen through. We didn't worry too much about such things, usually finding adequate sleeping accommodations on short notice wherever we went.

The political atmosphere in Jamaica in the '80s reminded us of the hippie era of the '60s in the United States. The country's reggae musicians and political protests prompted Rudy and me to remark, "Just like home." We had heard of the reggae musicians and the dreadlocks groups, but encountering the social unrest in remote tropical areas came as something of a shock.

Rudy's response: "Nothing to fear; they're nice, Char." (He had used the same remark to me when a group of baboons accompanied us on a stroll through the countryside in Victoria Falls, Africa.)

Each time we took off from our guesthouse, our hostess warned, "Don't go into Kingston, and do stay on the main roads." As she waved goodbye, her expression was often that of a worried parent seeing her teenager off on his or her first date. Even our oldest son had warned us as we departed San Francisco Airport: "Don't you two go around talking to just anyone."

We drove around looking for schools in which to plant our Paintbrush Diplomacy seeds, as our anticipated call from Virus had not come through. Every day in our explorations we fell more deeply in love with the tropical fern groves, the casual Jamaican lifestyle, the English-flavored speech. The Caribbean climate is a far cry from San Francisco's. As we became warmer, our thirst grew.

When we travel, we never drink the water. Not being a big water drinker, this doesn't throw me too much. Of German roots, Rudy finds no pain in consuming beer. Thanks to his background, we made our first unexpected contact. Rudy spotted a tiny thatch-roofed stand selling cold drinks and goodies, and expressed a sentiment I've heard the world over, "A cold beer beckons, Char."

We eased into a seat at a small counter of the goody stand. On Rudy's left, sat a young Jamaican man in white shorts, white cotton hat, and Clorox-white shoes. Checking out our jeans and shoes, he asked, "Where are you folks from?"

We have been told all over the world that U.S. shoes are a tip-off to where we are from, but when we said we were from San Francisco, that was the usual sure-fire beginning to conversation the world over. As luck would have it, our young companion turned out to be a high-school teacher on spring break.

By the time we quenched our thirst, we had become pretty well acquainted with our new friend Rob. Explaining our program and relating our experiences whetted his interest. Finally, his squeaky-clean white tennis shoes made a little musical rhythm as he jumped up from his stool and suggested enthusiastically, "I can take you to a teaching chum of mine who is principal of a nearby secondary school!"

Rudy was all for getting into Rob's car right then, but I insisted we follow. "Artists are supposed to be more carefree than engineers," I tell Rudy as I feel our son's warning breath in my ear, "but being kidnapped in our old age would only lead to talk like 'I told you so!'"

Through a dense forest mile after mile with no sign of civilization, I began to wonder if we might be on a wild goose chase. A few tin shacks appeared on the horizon. Our leader motioned us up a small hill. More shacks appeared and we stopped in front of one. Out came a young woman holding her tiny baby, who was wearing a bright blue dress and matching hair ribbon, taped to a slightly emerging cap of black curls. An older woman lingered behind.

Rob greeted them as we approached their porch. "I have brought fine American visitors to meet William. Is he about? William and I were chums in teachers' college," he explained. "My name is Rob, and our guests are Char and Rudy Pribuss from San Francisco, California."

This left our new acquaintances with expressions no less amazed than if Rob were introducing us as space creatures.

We sat on their porch explaining our desire to bring a gift of American student art to a school in exchange for Jamaican student art. The older woman, William's mother and an ex-schoolteacher, listened intently as we once more described bene-fits to students throughout the world for the past 8 years. "A trade of letters and school pictures among the world's young will someday make them all more closely

Canada Age 4

Canada Age 10

Chile Age 7

Chile Age 6

Chile Age 12

Chile Age 9

Chile Age 11

Chile Age 11

Chile Age 12

China Age 15

China Age 8

China Age 7

China Age 12

China Age 12

China Age 17

China Age 16

China Age 16

China Age 16

China Age 16

China Age 15

China Age 15

China Age 12

China Age 15

China Age 13

Columbia Age 8

Czech Republic Age 5

Czech Republic Age 12

Czech Republic Age 12

Denmark Age 9

Denmark Age 10

E. Germany Age 12

E. Germany Age 11

E. Germany Age 9

E. Germany Age 11

E. Germany Age 12

Ecuador Age 12

Ecuador Age 6

related as adults," we urged. "With the help of your son and other Jamaican teachers, this dream could become a new possibility."

"I'm sorry," she said, "William is not here right now. School is over for Easter vacation, but I believe there might be some student art that I know William would like you to take."

From a small compartment she took some art of William's students—including portraits of two school musicians. We brought our gift to her. The art ranged from small children's Mickey Mouse paintings to rock star paintings by high-school students. Our new friends were delighted.

As I held up each painting in this small tin abode, I found myself looking at our young U.S. students' art with new eyes. From kindergarten to high school, I saw innovation and diversity ranging from collages using newspaper, to cloth and even sand over rubber cement. This inventiveness is truly America, I realized. Later I told Rudy, "This is one of our people's greatest strengths—trying the untried, seldom building on the old but starting from scratch and going for broke."

Before we left, we asked where we might attend a church service, as the following day was Good Friday. They told us of a general area to explore. As we left, Rudy gave the young woman something with which to buy the baby an Easter dress from us. Both women looked very pleased, but anxious to make a return offering. She asked shyly, "Would you like to hold the baby?"

I reached forward and accepted her tiny brown bundle for the magic that babies are. The room took on an atmosphere of joy I will never forget. No one spoke. Words can be such a deterrent to emotions.

The next day we located the area where our new friend had suggested a Good Friday service. We parked in a church lot but saw very few occupied spaces. Entering the church, we saw only one, but heard beautiful organ music drifting down from the organ loft. The custodian smiled as we left, indicating a line of people dressed in their Sunday best weaving their way into a wooded area. Although not as well dressed and the only whites, we joined the procession, bringing up the rear. Finally we reached a clearing with a stream nearby. "Too bad there isn't a cold drink goody stand," Rudy teased as we dripped in perspiration.

"Quiet, Rudy!" I whispered. "This is a church-oriented situation, I think. When in a church service near a stream in Jamaica, do as the Jamaicans."

"Right." A wonderful chorus resounded from the people bordering the stream. Hymn books were passed out. We received them gratefully, as this appeared to be a religion with which we were not familiar. Singing along, we felt very close to those around us. Warmth both spiritual and bodily enveloped us. As so often happens in our unplanned experiences of this kind, we felt a little detached from ourselves— as if participating in a play, but more as part of the audience than a player.

Before we knew it, we witnessed a baptism of young adults in white clothing being fully immersed in the lake stream. We no longer felt our difference. The joy and reverence of these people enveloped us. When the service ended, we asked the minister if the newly baptized would like us to take their pictures. All lined up with beaming faces. We promised to send them prints upon our return home.

Believing we had been observant of Good Friday in a very special way, we were about to return to our car when the minister approached us. "Our Good Friday service will now take place in the church," he told us. "We would be much honored to have you both attend."

How could we say, "We don't belong to your church; we're only visitors"? We accepted.

Rudy and I drifted into the church, which was packed with children and adults, all looking starched and unaffected by the humidity. White fans hummed—we continued to drip. Women and girls were straw-hatted and gloved. Men wore suits and neckties. Rudy and I looked like a couple of laid-back, dripping Californians. We sat in the rear of the church and realized, for the first time, what it felt like to belong to an ethnic minority.

The minister gave a fine sermon; several visiting ministers did the same. Finally it was announced that there were two visitors who had come "a long mile." All eyes turned to Rudy and me as the pastor asked us to rise and receive the congratulations and applause. We had never felt so honored for so little.

When we left the church three hours later, people shyly approached and asked us to come to their homes and share whatever they had to offer. We had quantities of tropical juice of every kind—no way to have juice from one and not accept from another. When it was time to leave, I could hear myself splash.

That night our solicitous guesthouse owner invited us to join her dinner party for the campaign manager of the new candidate running for prime minister; other politically minded Jamaicans would be in attendance as well. Would we join them? Our hostess looked so imploringly at us that a "yes" was the only possible answer. At this point, the most we knew about Jamaica was how a baptism in a stream was conducted. We explained our ignorance, but she would not hear of this as a reason for declining her invitation.

The party was a wonderful experience. We learned that politics in Jamaica was not too different from politics in most areas of the world. We listened. We have seen so many similar times where people seek answers to the world's problems through the perfect leader, but as far as I know, no such person has yet arrived on this earth. We came away glad to know we were just Paintbrush Diplomats.

What ever happened to Virus? Since we had been put up at a guesthouse different from the one originally planned, she had to do some scrounging to find us. When we finally met on the front porch, it was as if we were long-lost friends. Virus had been well versed on our exploits by our friend Ann, but we never knew quite how detailed her knowledge was. She had newspaper articles about us as well as our picture.

She took us to her school, showing off her classroom with great pride. Student art all along the walls promptly became ours as we presented her with our U.S. gift. Unfortunately, her children were on Easter vacation, but this visit was the beginning of a strong connection by mail over the years.

At home, we did not keep in touch with Jamaican politics, never saw another baptism in a river, and never again found a thatched goody stand or another potential Paintbrush Diplomat with the Jamaican charm of Rob, but we won't forget any of our experience. How long can we say, "Virus, we love you," but we do.

Did we ever see all the scenic points of interest my TV tells me Jamaica offers? Probably not. Yet we met, hugged, and were nurtured by Jamaican people. Many young people in their country and ours know a little more about each other as a result of our program, and we could write a Jamaican travel folder uniquely our own.

Waving goodbye, I no longer was apprehensive about where we would go next. Many of the neighbors had somehow heard of our visit, and all insisted we stop by their home for a cool drink. Complying with all, we splashed our way back to the car. I no longer worried about where we were going.

"We're on the right road!" I said to Rudy as we drove away.

WARM HEARTS IN A COLD CLIMATE

Alaska—1980

Chester and Helen Kotzebue

Going about as far north as my imagination could envision, we flew to the Arctic zone when our pilot announced, "Fasten your seat belts, we are crossing the Arctic line."

Suddenly the plane took a lurch upward, then a sudden downward jolt. We both hooked up. A tremulous flyer like me doesn't need a comic for a pilot. Kotzebue in the Arctic zone made us wonder if we were truly still part of the America we came from.

"Where are the dog sleds?" I asked. The engine buzz meant that no one heard my innocent question. I wanted to meet the real Eskimo people. Where were they, I wondered, half-awake with "midnight sun" timing.

Young Eskimo men raced everywhere in their snowmobiles. The beach was filled with salmon fishermen and boats. Racks and racks of drying fish formed a mosaic for as far as the eye could see, and the air was permeated with a not too pleasant reminder of my childhood days with cod liver oil.

How do you go up to an Eskimo washing his snowmobile and say, "Would you like to feel closer to what you call the Lower 48 through our Paintbrush Diplomacy program? Where is your school?" Or, the most ignorant of all, "Could we visit your igloo?" We soon learned that *that* image went out with old movies like *Nanook of the North*. Their wood-framed houses were not palatial but quite adequate for their present lifestyle.

My first encounter with a native came in the early morning at a coffee shop counter. He leaned close to me, peering into my pale blue eyes with his narrow black ones.

"Where are you from?"

At the mention of California, he smiled with what now seemed like nearly closed eyes, his perfect white teeth accentuated by his slightly darker skin.

"Oh, I was in the Army at Fort Ord. It's my favorite place in the world!"

I meditated on what this experience must have been for him, exchanging his cold white earth for the endless sand of Fort Ord. When I told him of my interest in the migration of the Mongol people and possible connection with the Eskimo and American Indian cultures, he squinted his eyes even more and, with a disgruntled look, said:

"We don't like those guys, they have funny eyes."

I didn't dare mention the old adage about the pot calling the kettle black. After all, Rudy and I were trying to bring people together, and comparisons could unearth a whole other kettle of fish. Speaking of fish, Rudy got into another eye-opener when our friend explained about the Eskimo fishing rights in certain areas and how wealthy some of his people had become as a result. Too bad so many of the world's cultures deal in taking away and dividing up another's land, losing old cultural practices in the process.

The next day being thrown in the air in the "blanket toss," we were told how this ancient custom was used to get a better look at the distant horizon in order to prepare for possible danger. As I dodged an approaching snowmobile after climbing out of the blanket, I realized how far the young Eskimo was from the world his elders would like to preserve. We were informed that high-school students, flown to schools "outside" or to the Lower 48, rarely fully returned to the blanket toss.

Our hotel manager told us we might need a good sleep to arm ourselves for the trip to Nome, Anchorage, and finally Fairbanks. How right he was! Connections were not easy, and it took all day. Seeing the Alaskan pipeline was quite overwhelming as an engineering feat, but even then we didn't feel convinced about the effect this would have on the animals. History proved, to our sorrow, how right we were in being apprehensive.

At each stop the Alaskan people were always so open and friendly that we loved meeting and talking with them. They all seemed to have networks throughout the state, sending friends to meet other friends, like an extended family. The media often knew our whereabouts. We had no trouble making contacts from then on.

Arriving in Fairbanks, we had a message from a local newspaper asking for an interview. "News must be sparse in these parts," we told each other. We agreed, having no idea they would be in our room in the next few minutes. Vanity has become a luxury I can no longer afford. Television interviews have never led to movie offers anyway.

The next day we rented a car and set out, with Rudy announcing, in between his racking chest coughs, "This weather may be better for Eskimos than for us."

When his condition worsened, I took over the driving and finally pulled up in a tiny town near Homer.

"When you're sick you need a doctor," I announced in spite of his protests. Entering the waiting room of a general practitioner's office, we were confronted with a room filled with young expectant mothers.

"A doctor's a doctor," I whispered, as the young women laughed. After a thorough examination and a diagnosis of viral pneumonia, we acquired a bottle of huge pink pills fit for a reindeer. Getting on our way with a promise to check with a doctor in Juneau, we felt more confident, until Rudy was overcome by violent hiccups and stomach upset.

In our Juneau hotel, I tried desperately to remember every home remedy I knew to stop Rudy's new malady. Supported by the corner of the room, he wound up standing on his head at my request. With his methodical, time-oriented brain, he asked in between hiccups, "What time is it?"

I strapped his wristwatch to his ankle. In desperation, we both started to laugh. His hiccups stopped. We were driven on by our Paintbrush Diplomacy addiction.

We had been referred by an Indian girl to the Head Start program in Juneau. We met Judy Franklet and discussed an art exchange between the Tlingit Indian schools and our contact with the Taos, New Mexico, Hopi and Navajo Indian students. With our enthusiasm brimming over, Rudy and I were like two children. All we needed was a full staff of volunteers and an unlimited supply of money to connect every young person in the world with our Paintbrush Diplomacy.

Meeting young Robbie Benko, Juneau State Museum's assistant director, we felt even more encouraged. This enthusiastic woman showed us their state flag— designed by a young Alaskan boy of 13. Its seven gold stars represent Alaska's gold-mining industry in the form of the Big Dipper, and an eighth star in the corner represents the North Star, symbolizing the state's location in the far north. When we were told this story of the flag's young designer, we immediately launched into our children's program as Robbie listened intently. She insisted on coming to our hotel to see the art portfolio we carried containing our children's art treasures.

"Hey, you guys," she exclaimed in a true Alaskan last-frontier manner, "how about having me connect the Lower 48 with the 49th state?" We heard this expression, Lower 48, more than once, indicating that our fellow-citizens to the north did not always feel completely connected with us. Robbie explained about some of the remote areas where schoolchildren received their school programs when bush pilots flew the work in on a regular basis. We were given some impressive art from these schools.

Robbie kept her every promise, along with insisting that we stay with her parents in North Carolina when we followed the art we had lent to the Smithsonian Institution for its tour of the United States that next year. We took much of the Alaskan student art to India and some to Hawaii, where the Hawaiian children couldn't imagine why the Eskimo paintings showed children in fur-trimmed hats and mittens. Who could, if they had never seen snow? "Americans need to know a little more about each other," we told them.

Our final Alaskan flight was to Sitka, where we delivered the remaining California art and program information to a principal there. These arrangements had been made for us, but we were not quite sure by whom. A note in our hotel box explained all. A last news interview was also arranged. Somehow, everything went well, just in time for us to grab our three-day ferry ride down the Alaskan

Inlet. Sitting on the deck in the sun, resting our bodies against the ship's side and watching the little islands roll by, provided a much-needed tonic. We were the oldest people on this voyage, surrounded by young adventurers who lived on deck with sleeping bags, tents, and pots and pans for cooking. Some even had dogs housed on the lower deck.

"Too bad our generation wasn't able to grab life like this when we were young," Rudy said. "We would have been in our tent right now with these kids."

"Sure," I said, "but right now my old back cries at the thought. Besides, I wonder if this group will be doing as well as we are when they have children."

Once home, we sent the Taos Indians a huge painting of a whole city done by the children of the Arctic, and we gave as much coverage as we could to these wonderful, loving people in the warmest cold areas we've ever visited.

Did we marvel over the glaciers, Mt. McKinley, and the reenactment of the Gold Rush days? As we say when returning from all parts of the world, "Yes, but not as much as we loved building relationships with the world's people through Paintbrush Diplomacy."

THE COLORFUL STATE

Hawaii—1982

Hawaiian Breeze

The Hawaiian island of Kauai, the Garden Island, gets the most rainfall of all the islands in this beautiful archipelago—offering a year-round botanical treat.

Our trip for Paintbrush Diplomacy in 1982 was a nostalgic reminder of our first trip to Hawaii, when we took our children; we had no business doing it, no money to pay for it. We had taken them across the United States and to Canada in the same way, and now to this wonderful paradise. I can still remember making for myself and the girls cotton coats, each a different pastel color, and cotton flowered mu-mus from the same bolt of on-sale fabric. Together we were a threesome to stop traffic, and the price was right.

On this current trip alone with Rudy, only our foreign children's art, and the hope that our Paintbrush Diplomacy would be interesting to Hawaiian school-children, accompanied us. After settling in—a day at the beach, a day at the pool breathing the fumes of too-sweet suntan lotion, hearing where everyone had been, watching everyone checking out everyone else—I could see Rudy's restlessness start to build. At such times, he reminded me of a lion pacing back and forth in its cage.

"Tomorrow's the day," I said. "Let's give the Hawaiians a try, but where to begin?" In such cases, it was always the greatest of adventures—no idea where we could plant our seeds. When we had resorted to embassy help in the "difficult" countries, we badly needed it and were grateful for it. The experiences that we started from scratch were the ones we most enjoy remembering. In this case, the light Hawaiian rain we started to encounter might have beaten us. Instead, we went to a department store, bought plastic yardage in which to wrap our portfolio and ourselves, and headed for the nearest school. Once there, following our usual procedure, we went to the office and asked for the principal.

Walking into a school wrapped in plastic with water running off our noses could be enough to shock anyone, but the little Hawaiian secretary, like the rest of the hospitable Hawaiian people, politely asked if she could help us.

"Yes," we said, unwrapping our art portfolio, "Could we see your principal? We would like to tell him of our children's international art and letter exchange program."

"He may be in a meeting," she smiled, "but I will tell him you are here." She probably wanted to prepare him for possible aliens from another world. We sat down in an office similar to those we've seen all over the world—saw many of the same things we have also seen all over the world. In this one, there were a couple of children with large brown eyes who sat in the corner—behavior problems or under-the-weather cases waiting for mother, or just waiting.

On the walls, hung children's art depicting scenes of the rolling blue Pacific with surfers, Hawaiian dancers, and of course, palm trees with coconuts. A couple of young teachers passed through with coffee cups (Kona coffee, we presumed). Finally the smiling young Hawaiian principal arrived.

Rudy usually started the conversation with something like, "We are from San Francisco. My wife and I have a collection of foreign children's art, acquired in our travels while exchanging United States student art in foreign schools. We would love to share them with and talk to your students, hoping they would like to join our Paintbrush Diplomacy program, which fosters understanding among the world's children." We then show the principal what we have brought. This always paves the way. Who can ever resist children's art?

Often the conversation simply gets around to things like "Whom do you work for?" or "Who sponsors you?" When we tell them that we work for no one, that we save for a trip each year, that Rudy is an engineer and I an art teacher and artist, they feel a little more confident.

I finish our informal introduction by explaining that we like to think our efforts may make the young know and understand each other so that they will do a better job than some of us in running this world when their turn comes.

With no further discussion, this principal said, "A class is about to end. If you can wait about 10 minutes more, Miss Haole will show you to our fourth grade class."

"We're on," we remarked, smiling at each other. The 10 minutes went fast. We never have a prepared script, but as we entered the class of sun-scrubbed Hawaiian fourth-graders, our adrenal juices started flowing, and we felt fully alive.

The class loved our art. However, it would have to send us theirs as they were unprepared, and we could not stay longer than two more days. This was no problem. We were U.S. neighbors, and although we sometimes complain of our mail service, we know that it looks good compared to some we have dealt with.

A little encouragement goes a long way. After this first encounter, we tried another school. Millie Wellington, the next teacher we met, made you wish she could show up every Monday morning to light up your life and make you forget it was Monday. She smiled, showing perfect white teeth. Her black eyes always made her look as if she were laughing. It didn't take long to convince her that ours was a good idea. She showed us murals of beach scenes that her children had painted on the school building. "They can pretend they are at the beach for a little while during recess," she said, laughing.

We went to a classroom in her school and watched her students paint after we talked to them and showed them paintings of their peers from around the world. A number of them painted bright-colored dinosaurs. One little boy painted a purple unicorn. Others did what one would expect from Hawaiian children—surfers and palm trees—but in such bright colors that we remarked to each other how children in moderate and hot climates do make brighter-colored art.

Nearly all children also paint the sun, but only in a U.S. school did we receive a painting with the sun showing a huge smile with one cavity in its front tooth. No one can deny our originality! All their paintings were offered to us. We promised to send Millie a Paintbrush Diplomacy art collection to be shown in the state office building in Kauai.

When we got home, time went by, and as is often the case while waiting for art from a recent stop, we wondered if the school would really send the art. Hand carrying and delivering is always best. Art finally arrived from the first Hawaiian class. Our excitement was the same as always.

"Look at this," I enthused, bringing Rudy a roll of art done on simulated tapa cloth. The Hawaiian students in School #1 did their art on brown paper, emulating the medium used in early days. Tapa cloth was then made from thin, beaten bark, but this brown paper copy looked like the real thing to us.

On our next trip, which was to India, the children marveled at the Hawaiian children's art, feeling the rumpled surfaces of the "tapa cloth," becoming ecstatic over the gorgeous bright-colored monster paintings. Little did we know when we started for the first Hawaiian school, wrapped up like plastic mummies, that we were beginning an exposure of Hawaiian children to those of India. The adventuresome spirit is the name of the game—plus always remembering you have nothing to lose—your gain could be something wonderful, although you may never know for sure.

It would be easy for the reader to assume that, as it often does in a youthful love affair, our enthusiasm would wear thin. No chance. We became even more addicted to Paintbrush Diplomacy with each new encounter.

Without once trying our dream for themselves, travelers will never know the fun they're missing if they don't get a handle on our paintbrush. Grab hold!

INDIA AND NEIGHBORS

New Delhi, Bombay, Kerala, Sri Lanka, Kashmir, Nepal, Bhutan—1982

New Delhi Woman

Many well-traveled people tell me they would not go to India. The poverty, the masses of people, the cows being treated like people, and the possibility of contracting a serious illness make them wince and point their sights in other directions. Their loss.

Before going to India, fate took us to a dinner party hosted by my art mentor, Leonard Breger, where we met close friends of San Francisco's Indian consul and his wife, Ishrat and Narsima Aziz. We were asked to an Indian restaurant where we ate desserts covered with silver leaf, listened to mesmerizing Indian music, and found ourselves drifting toward visions of the Taj Mahal bathed in moonlight. It didn't take too much mesmerizing.

Rudy thought that, by now, we could travel on our own, but I felt that going to such an area alone at our age might be "asking for it," so we signed up with a tour. As usual, it proved a mixed blessing. On the one hand, our group leader found us contacts we probably could not have obtained by beating the bush on our own. On the other hand, however, the way things developed, we would have been just as well off taking our chances.

New Delhi was our first stop, an introduction to the grim realities of everyday life in India. I can still remember the bus driver saying, "We will be out for a half-day only. Adjust slowly." One woman didn't, and after viewing the street confusion, the beggars, and people transporting a dead body down an alley, she took the first flight back to the States.

Doing homework on India before leaving was a great help. Also, we had the benefit of correspondence with contacts of India's consul in San Francisco and his wife. She became a true friend to me—a great advocate for Paintbrush Diplomacy. The Rotarians had also set up contacts, and a doctor friend of Rudy showed us slides from his recent trip. He and his wife, also a doctor, kindly got us every necessary prescription medication in the pharmacy.

In New Delhi we pulled away from our group activities for a few days to visit the Shankar children's center. Ready to set out for the meeting with the center's director, we soon discovered that things were always closed for Hindu, Moslem, and Buddhist holidays, government celebrations, or never-ending festivals. On one occasion we decided to spend the day in our room sorting our art for stops in New Delhi schools and cultural centers. With our hotel floor and bed covered with art, a reporter called from India's answer to *Life* magazine. If convenient, she would be out directly for an interview.

When I opened the door to her, my eyes were glued to her feet—bare, her toes covered with ruby and emerald rings. Very tall, Chandra Lother was well worth tipping my head back to take in her full dramatic appearance. Her silken sari of brilliant fuchsia was edged in gold, enhanced—maybe even upstaged—by the fuchsia dot between her eyebrows and the diamond in her nostril. How unworthy I felt in my California cotton shift and sandals! "I should be interviewing you!" I exclaimed.

She proved to be totally enchanting, entertaining us with stories of Indian festivals. Our stories seemed pale by comparison, but she took copious notes and photos, promising to send the magazine as soon as the article appeared. It never came. (Our experience with the Indian mail system answers why.) Chandra's voice modulated up and down as she spoke, her flashing black eyes and gorgeous silken body made unimportant such things as Indian envelopes that didn't stick, coins that didn't work in pay phones, phone connections that often didn't connect. However, sometimes I noticed Rudy's teeth clench. San Francisco businessmen expect more.

Finally the Shankar children's center ignored one of the endless holidays and opened its doors just for us, rewarding us for our patience. Our tour of their center revealed every kind of program encouraging children with the arts. Many poor children enjoyed its library of books printed on recycled paper. Annual international art contests offered the winner a gold coin and a trip to another country. We left their art coordinator with our art and tried to undo a little of the indifferent image they had of American students. Leaving with as many contest entry blanks as they gave us, we promised to spread the word back home, which we have done.

Now to rejoin the group in Kerala, Southwest India. One quick air stop between New Delhi and Kerala—Bombay—proved fatal. If Rudy were Tony Bennett, he could compose a sequel to "I Left My Heart in San Francisco," called "I Left My Underwear in Bombay, and Then Some." He was wiped out, as we say in the States. One suitcase each we took in, and out we came with just mine. Rudy, in his usual businesslike manner, went right to airport authorities. This was our first encounter with what we began referring to as the "nirvana approach" on the part of the airline representative, not on ours. East now showed West how "never the twain shall meet" came about.

Down but not out, we proceeded to Kerala, Rudy wearing an outfit I would come to know intimately as the weeks passed. When we landed at the airport in

Kerala, we were met by two white-robed Indian Catholic priests in black berets. Our priest in San Mateo, Father Kristy Daniles, had made the connection. His brethren took us in like long-lost sheep, especially when we explained our loss. Clothes were the least of it. Camera, contact papers, some medication, slides—all were no more. The priests' best efforts and prayers proved futile.

Our delivery to the Kerala grade school occurred immediately following our arrival. Apparently the children had long awaited our coming. A shower and change would have helped us, in spite of the fact that Rudy had nothing to change into, but we didn't want to keep the children waiting. The weather was terribly warm. Our clothes stuck to us although it had just stopped raining.

We were shown to a schoolyard filled with red-uniformed children enveloped in steam. At first they were quite shy and maintained the behavior that nuns the world over impose. (We don't put this down, as some schools prove so uninhibited that two grandparents can get trampled to death when recess bells ring!)

The formality did not last long, however. Their beautiful dark eyes focused on us expectantly and I called out, "Hello!" The hello of Indians, who learn English from the British, sounds more like "hallo" to a Californian. Soon the whole playground reverberated with their melodic "hallos." Rudy and I leaned down and hugged them, and my emotional French/Irish background brought tears to my eyes.

We were next ushered into the nuns' quarters, where the good ladies offered us their beds, to rest up from the long trip and the heat, and a bowl of cashew nuts and tea. Peel anything, we had been warned, a dictum not to be fooled with. But not wanting to hurt the feelings of the nuns seemed worth dying for, so we ate their offering and thanked them.

Next we joined the children in the auditorium, where they had their art ready for us. These eight- and nine-year-olds had such beautiful, carefully matted work waiting that we felt we could never give enough in return. When we brought out work from our Hawaiian children made of simulated tapa cloth, paintings from San Francisco students of skate boarders wearing Adidas running shoes and sports jock jackets, we almost brought the house down. Drawings of U.S. cartoon characters evoked cries of "Oh, Snoopy" or "Mickey" or "Superman." We were emotionally overwhelmed, as we always are anywhere in the world when we feel people, even little ones, coming closer together through our efforts.

Our tour group, now taking compassion on Rudy, started offering such things as a pair of socks (never found these in stores), a T-shirt, or whatever they could spare. My late night washing did not always dry by morning. One night, to speed the drying process, I hung Rudy's jockey shorts over a light bulb, resulting in burnt "lace" underpants from then on. As our next stop was Sri Lanka, where the humidity was even worse, I convinced Rudy I did him a favor by aerating his undies. He took it like the sport of sports.

Kandy, Sri Lanka, was both a joy and a challenge. First the challenge. The day before we were scheduled to visit a school for all ages, I did something to my leg while stepping down from the steep last step of our bus. "Ouch!" Deep down I knew I would have to cope with the pain, even if I had to crawl on my hands and knees.

That night in our hotel I took turns soaking my leg in ice cubes and crawling to an alternate soaking of hot water in the tub. Rudy had gone with the group, at my insistence, to see Buddha's tooth. Better than looking at my leg, I told him. It now looked like the mother of the other leg.

Before going, Rudy did his now almost religious ritual of placing a call to the last airport, telling of our new destination, just in case the luggage showed up. That night—tucked safely under mosquito netting with me pretending I was an exotic siren in an old B movie—emphatic banging on our door suddenly awakened us. "Oh please sir, telephone," came from a very polite but excited voice.

Rudy, once a pajama man, was now back to Mother Nature since our loss. I will always remember him dashing out the door in this condition, with the determined look of a hunter stalking his prey. On his return, he murmured, "I arrived just in time for the wire to go dead." I could have laughed, but the marriage had lasted too long for that test.

I arose the next morning with both legs operating pretty well, to my surprise. The school to which we were delivered was filled to the breaking point with high-school students in uniform and teachers acting as if Hollywood celebrities had arrived. This was hard for us to understand, considering the condition we were in. With a little mingling after our Paintbrush Diplomacy presentation, we realized they were thrilled to have people from the United States give their time and bring gifts.

No one wanting to be excluded, they literally tore their outstanding art from the walls. Just getting something of themselves to the States seemed a thrill. One eighth-grade boy asked for my signature and phone number. What an "upper"! Since our return, their art has gone to shows at the San Francisco City Hall, the Cannon Rotunda in Washington, D.C., San Francisco International Airport, and far too many California schools to mention.

On to Srinagar, and our stay on a houseboat! The Vale of Kashmir was comparable only to Joseph Conrad's *Lost Horizon*. "Other worldliness" came to mind. The people were from a very unique and proud culture—mostly Moslem—often identifying more with Pakistan than India in their political viewpoint.

To show our appreciation for all the trouble students and teachers had taken to get our art exchange working, Rudy and I decided to give a tea party for them on our houseboat. Mr. Khan, our guide, made the necessary arrangements. Most of the children had never been on these tourist houseboats. They arrived by small canoes, wearing their best and bringing art different from any we had seen so far. Many were illustrations of their fables.

We were almost reluctant to give them our carefree California student art. They loved it, however, almost as much as the tea party. Our travel group sat in for our talk, and we found a couple of Paintbrush Diplomacy recruits for their next trip. If travelers only knew what a "trip" our program is, they would never leave home without our rules for the game.

On to Nepal. Still many lingering American hippies appeared, but the look of this place had to wait while I shopped for a wool covering for Rudy's bald head

Ecuador Age 17

Ecuador Age 13

Ecuador Age 14

Ecuador Age 8

Ecuador Age 13

Ecuador Age 13

Ecuador Age 11

England Age 14

Estonia Age 10

Estonia Age 9

Estonia Age 10

Estonia Age 10

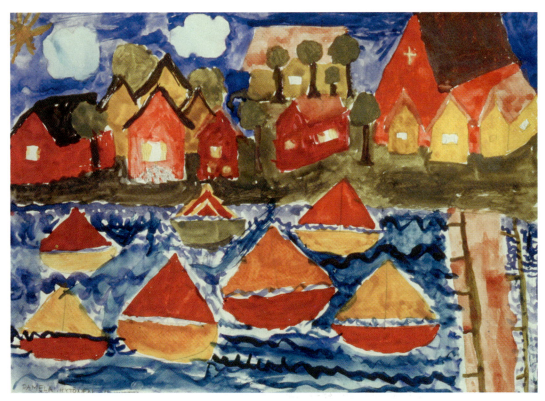

Finland Age 9

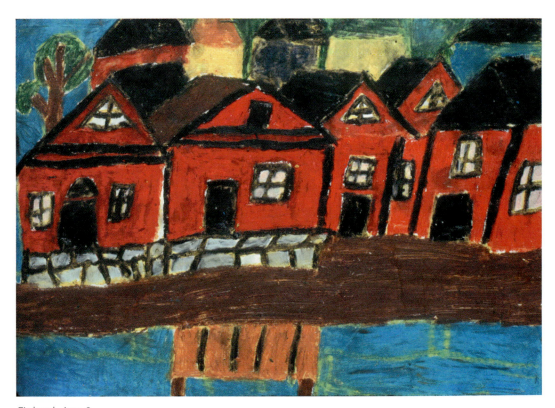

Finland Age 9

Finland Age 8

Haiti Age 12

Haiti Age 12

Hong Kong Age 14

Hungary Age 12

Hungary Age 9

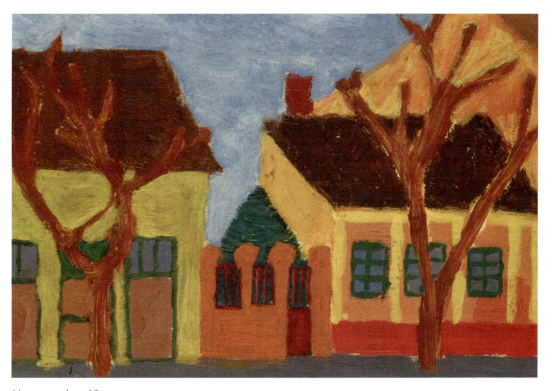

Hungary Age 13

Hungary Age 13

Hungary Age 12

Hungary Age 14

Hungary Age 14

Iceland Age 10

Iceland Age 10

India Age 12

India Age 14

India Age 9

India Age 8

India Age 11

India Age 13

India Age 14

India Age 14

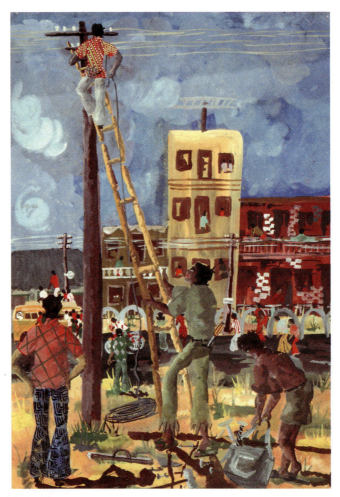

India Age 14

India Age 12

and freezing body. The English schoolboy-type shorts that a tailor had made at our last stop just wouldn't do. With what seemed like a 200-pound sweater and a great knit hat, he could have passed for one of Sir Edmund Hillary's mountain-climbing buddies.

We were off and running once more, but starting to show a slower pace. Our hotel on top of a hill was archaic, mysteriously beautiful, and freezing. Since we were near the base of the Himalayan Mountains, the view helped us forget some of the cold. Tiny coolie women carried our luggage up the hill on their narrow backs. We must not interfere. They needed the money. Since we had lost our list of contacts along with the luggage, you can imagine our surprise when we were being paged for a phone call from an Indian Rotarian. Exhilarating stuff, this.

The next day, our Rotarian friend brought us to a Canadian Jesuit teacher in a boys' school. We arranged to have his student musicians do a concert at our hotel the following night. If it weren't for a special after-school program offered by Father Roberts, the boys would have followed in the footsteps of their coolie mothers who carried our luggage. The musicians arrived in a hotel they had never set foot in, instruments in hand, all in some kind of necktie and jacket. A Mozart treat ensued, and there wasn't a dry eye in the house. All that the boys lacked was a cello, so our group decided to take up a collection for them to buy one. We hear that the orchestra is now complete. We also trade art on a yearly basis with these many-talented students.

Our group was now showing signs of wear. Such luxuries as bouffant hairdos were long gone. Only the brave accepted an offer to go on to Bhutan for an extra week. In spite of travel sickness, a pulled ligament, and no replacement available for Rudy's hearing aid, Rudy and I still persisted in not missing a thing. Even more important, we still had ten U.S. student paintings we could not waste.

So, King Jigme Wangchuk of Bhutan, here we come! Our guide, Maria Scheeley, managed to get an appointment for us in a school right out of *The King and I* movie. The headmistress had come from England to teach the children of the royal family. She wound up marrying a Bhutanese, had three children, and was instrumental in forming the public school where we would speak. The kinder-garten children there gave us art I would not trade for anything in the Louvre. Completely enchanting!

The headmistress said, "Please return when we are not testing, and we can give you more of our art gifts." I was amused, as she made it seem as simple as going to our local market. In reality, it was one of our most hair-raising journeys—on winding, narrow mountain roads. There were no guardrails, and when I was brave enough to look down, my stomach dropped where my eyes led it. The teacher took many pieces of the Bhutanese students' art from the walls, and the generous students wanted us to take something from each of them to bring to "the big country."

We will never forget this fairy tale kingdom in the clouds, their Buddhist monasteries that seemed to attach to the mountain peaks through prayer alone, or their young king, Jigme Wangchuk, playing basketball with his subjects. We were told we might meet with him that day but unfortunately something important had come up. Playing basketball *was* important, we decided.

"Smart king," I mused, "he doesn't need votes, but he knows playing ball with his subjects is the name of the game."

Back at Bombay's airport, Rudy made one more futile attempt at locating his lost luggage before flying home. With a faraway look in his eye, the airport director gave a response we had heard many times, "If it is to be, you will find it."

I suppose it wasn't meant to be, but we gained a great deal more than we lost and would return again tomorrow if offered the chance. This time, however, Rudy would put some extra clothing in his backpack, and I would take an extra supply of travel laundry soap. Clothes may make the man, but a true test of loving a mate is living with him for a whole month while he wears what no well-dressed man would be seen dead in, and yet never dream of switching.

SCANDINAVIAN CLASSROOMS JOIN THE CALIFORNIA MIX

Finland, Sweden, Denmark, Norway—1983

Glassblower Åsa and her husband Jan Brandt with Char and Rudy in Torshälla

Getting to Scandinavia in 1983 was a great feat. When I first suggested it, Rudy had balked a bit, offering his oft-used answer, "Let's save that area for the time when we are more doddering and have more money."

My response was, "I feel doddering enough already, and we never worried before about traveling without money."

I finally won out.

Finland, where we began our Scandinavian trip, came about mainly because of Vera Maki, an art friend and loyal supporter of Paintbrush Diplomacy since our struggling beginnings. (How can I not realize we are still struggling, and may always be?) Vera, born of Finnish parents, had taught her elderly father how to paint while he was in her care. Off to work, she left him with canvases, paints, brushes, and the message, "You can do it, Dad, and when I return I want to see it."

He did it, and so well that the Finns invited Vera to present her dad's work in a Helsinki art gallery. Vera, not young herself, responded with flying colors. She also made wonderful friends there and launched Rudy and me on our 1983 Paintbrush Diplomacy entrance. Thank you, Vera.

The Finnish people had a beauty in their art, as well as that of their children's, which had a uniqueness and mysterious quality to it, unlike art anywhere else in Scandinavia. They seemed to have woven their art from old myths and fables connected with their spirituality, which gave it a beautiful ethereal feeling. The Finnish Cultural Centers arranged for us to visit their children's art center, where they did a newspaper interview with us. Since it was summer, we were taken into an enchanting country setting, in which an old home was used for a children's art academy. Outdoor sculptures greeted us, made from whatever the children found—string, sticks, rope.

After presenting our children's art, we watched a young man from the United

States, Timothy Persons, supervise the construction of a children's ceramic kiln. Timothy turned out to be one of our more unexpected surprises. He was brought from the States to introduce young "new world" talent to the Finns' world-famous Arabia porcelain.

Nothing would do but that we enjoy a cultural tour with Timothy. Before we knew it, Rudy and I were in his all-purpose van heading for his work place, the Arabia factory. Gorgeous blue and white works of art merged with some of Timothy's very avant-garde creations. Traditional Finnish pieces enriched the mix.

Over a beer (naturally), it turned out that back in the States Tim had been dating a girl whose sister was dating our older son. Trading stories brought us quite close, and he insisted on cooking dinner for us in his apartment. What an adventure! His phone never stopped ringing, and finally one impatient girlfriend appeared in person. Rudy and I weren't too old yet to realize that our quick departure was in order, but not before we promised to get a message back to the girl he left behind.

Ah, youth! And especially in such a creative, outgoing society where one's artistic needs could be fulfilled without even pursuing them! "Don't tell me again, Rudy, how different our youth was. I don't want to hear it," I said, before he could say what I knew he was going to say.

Our next encounter was with a Finnish Rotarian, whom our dear friend George Kristovich, a Rotarian in the States, had contacted regarding our visit. He had done much letter writing in advance to his contacts before our various adventures. They never let us down. This one was no exception. A Finnish Rotarian brought art from a group of students who had participated with the Rotarians in a safety poster contest. As if this wasn't enough, our friend also insisted on treating us to a typical Finnish lunch of delicious seafood.

At this point, we learned that a Soviet ferry plied the waters of the Gulf of Finland between Helsinki and Tallinn (with a stop at Leningrad)—an opportunity for us to visit Estonia and Latvia. This sidetrip, beginning and ending in Helsinki, warrants a chapter unto itself, and I have described it in the following chapter.

Once back in Finland, we boarded a train for Sweden. Train rides were a way of reviewing our notes. Sometimes I could throw in a quick sketch of the landscape in our diary when we came to a loading zone. By the time we arrived at our first stop in Torshälla, Sweden, the rain had started coming down in sheets. We grabbed our thin travel raincoats from our backpacks and gathered up our gear. Looking at each other, we wondered who would want to claim us. Before leaving home, Rudy had received a rather vague message from Los Angeles, initiated by the helpful Swedish consul in San Francisco, but we didn't hold out much hope for a welcoming committee, especially at 9:00 p.m. in this rainstorm.

Wrong we were. As we stood on the dark train platform, a refreshing, rosy-cheeked version of Sweden's twin to English actor David Niven greeted us. He came toward us, introduced himself as Jan Brandt, quickly relieved us of some of our burdens, and led us to his car. His connection to our U.S. cultural center was due to his work with Torshälla's children's art community. Information about us had come to him via our San Francisco consul, relayed to the Los Angeles cultural representative of our project.

Upon arrival in Jan's home, we were welcomed by his lovely wife, Åsa, and their boys. His young sons were remarkably casual about our entrance into their beautiful, serene-looking home. After removing our shoes (everyone did), we were brought to our own wonderfully private room. Åsa, a glass blower of renown, had prepared one of her inimitable little vegetarian delights. Their home, with its white walls and polished wooden floors, was the backdrop for paintings, sculptures, and Åsa's beautiful glass creations. I didn't know where to look first.

The next morning, Jan took us to the Torshälla student art center, where we saw art history classes (children doing drawings of Torshälla's architectural history) and children composing and acting in their own theatrical productions. In one class, young students did tissue-paper collage portraits of their neighbor before beginning art class in order to know each other better and create more freely.

After our last talk in a Swedish school, we walked through a lovely tree-lined path to our bus with a group of blond heads following at a safe distance behind. While waiting for our bus, Rudy showed another young Jan (every boy seemed to be named this) the hand-slapping "high five" salute of our U.S. athletes. He loved it and imitated Rudy. When little blond Greta stood by Rudy, he reached out to give her a polite handshake, but she put her arms around his neck and kissed him. "I'll never be the same," he told me. Young Jan's last words: "Say hello to John Wayne for me, lady."

Even Sweden has labor strikes, we discovered. Hospitable Jan Brandt explained we might have trouble with seating on the train to Stockholm, which was indeed the case. All seats were taken except one facing the travelers, meant for a wheelchair person. "My body feels ready for this chair until I see a more worthy candidate," I told Rudy as I removed my backpack and settled in.

"Too bad you don't speak Swedish," Rudy said. You have a captive audience facing you and could tell them all about Paintbrush Diplomacy."

Arriving in Stockholm, we found our hotel mailbox bulging with letters. Rotarians had left phone numbers. The Swedish Cultural Center sent a representative who headed a children's art program called The Tree of Life, an organization also fostering art programs by children to achieve peace. Professor Anders Linders from the Swedish Institute brought us to their headquarters to see slides of a child's therapy program using art to unearth psychological damage in children. Most of the children treated were from those countries where war was a way of life.

Our last big surprise came in the form of a phone call from the sister of World War II hero, Raoul Wallenberg. We had brought art to Sweden from San Francisco's Raoul Wallenberg School. Wallenberg's sister was very touched by this. Our phone conversation was extremely moving. She still held out a slight hope that her brother's capture by the Russians had not ended in death. She kindly offered to send someone to pick up our art gift. If only the teacher from San Francisco's school, Diane Parkhill, and her young artists could have had this personal call and known the joy and appreciation they brought about through their caring art gift!

A friend whose cousin was a teacher in Copenhagen arranged our brief stop in Denmark. Marget, our contact, took us to her home and school, where her students gave us a rousing welcome. They were thrilled to receive our students' art gifts and, of course, anything depicting rock stars, athletes, or cartoon characters, regardless of language differences, seemed to link them with their foreign peers.

With only a short stopover in Oslo, Norway, our few hectic hours gave us time to see the show of artist Edvard Munch. Little did I know that we would be invited back, a few years later, to represent the United States at the opening of a children's museum.

Returning to Sweden, our departure for home was fast approaching, and our tiny Stockholm hotel room, looking like Grand Central Station for several days, was about to close up shop. After a final goodbye, Rudy admitted he loved our visit to Scandinavia as much as I did and hoped we could return, with or without money.

We sent Jan Brandt a Paintbrush Diplomacy exhibition, formerly shown in the main plaza of the United Nations. This was an international show that included some of the work acquired from Scandinavian students. He saw to its tour throughout Scandinavia. We consider Jan to be our Scandinavian representative for Paintbrush Diplomacy and hope our involvement through our children continues for many years.

Note to Jan, the little boy who wanted me to say hello to John Wayne for him:
I didn't have the heart to tell you that John Wayne had passed away a few years earlier, so I wouldn't be able to give him your message. I send you my apologies and Rudy sends you a high five.

OPENING THE DOOR A CRACK

Estonia and Latvia—1983

Ferryboat Ride

In 1983 our main trip was to Scandinavia, but the map told us we were just a short ferryboat ride from Finland to the communist world of Estonia. That was all it took for us to say, "Why not?" Unfortunately, maps don't measure ideological differences.

Leaving Finland and heading for Estonia on a Soviet ferryboat with red hammer and sickle flag flying behind us, I felt very adventurous. For a moment Rudy even seemed to have become James Bond. Laurel and Hardy couldn't have been less equipped to enter the beehive we were approaching.

Our ferryboat was furnished with a wonderful cafeteria and comfortable lounge, housing a conspicuous gold-framed painting of Lenin hanging above a rich brocade sofa. We were so taken in by it all that the transition from Finland to Leningrad (our required connecting link) went quickly. However, there was nothing quick about the "Red tape" we had to go through before resuming our journey to Estonia.

"Democracy, I already miss you," I whispered to Rudy.

"Cool it," he responded in an even lower whisper.

In Estonia's city of Tallinn, we were met by the Russian Friendship Society. This organization fostered cultural activities—high on the communist agenda. Three days before our arrival in Tallinn, a Korean passenger plane had been shot down by the Soviets over Russian territory, but we knew nothing about this as we were unable to read the Finnish newspapers and never seemed able to find a U.S. paper. (A breather from our news is sometimes the best part of the vacation. Not this time!)

Arrival in Tallinn revealed a world all its own—a unique and interesting country working hard to preserve its ethnic culture in spite of being under the blanket of the Soviets. We were welcomed with open arms, brought to their schools as well as to a children's art museum in an old home under renovation by Polish workmen. They explained that Poland, ravaged by war so often, produced the best workers for putting shattered buildings back together.

The Estonian people, like us, had no idea of the plane incident—blacked out on the news for five days.

We were treated like "good guys"—asked to be on a Soviet TV news slot surrounded by lovely children in red ties, enthusiastic educators, and government officials. Unfortunately, our large hotel, inhabited only by travelers, possessed three TV sets, all of which were out of order, "to be put right shortly" by Swedish technicians.

"I'll bet we were never shown on TV," Rudy grumbled. Only later, when some tourists told us they saw our program, did we change our tune. We couldn't have been more surprised.

An art friend, Erica Packman, who came from Riga, had motivated our visit to Latvia.

"Why would you *go* there, Charlotte?" she asked. "Nobody *goes* there; they only *leave* there, if they are lucky!" Nevertheless, I wanted to see her other world when we were that close.

In Latvia the news blackout had been lifted. We were made aware of the fact that our honeymoon with the Russian Friendship Society (also connected with the KGB) had come to an abrupt halt. They knew now of the airplane tragedy, and the Americans had become the "bad guys."

The Russian Friendship Society, we were told, headed up all cultural programs, and they would meet with us in the lobby of our hotel early in the morning. Promptly at 8:00 a.m. the Friendship committee arrived at our hotel reception desk. Something seemed different. The warm reception we saw on the faces of our Estonian friends didn't match the faces of our new acquaintances. We were ushered into a long black car, driven to an ominous-looking—probably once lavish—three-story home.

Up the stairs we were now brought into a large wood-paneled room where sliding carved wooden doors closed tightly behind us. Cozy? No! Chilling. Our "rights" as Americans seemed to have been detained on the other side of the door. Around a long, heavy, carved table we gathered—a government representative, a young woman interpreter, a blond American-looking and -speaking gentleman, and two American Paintbrush Diplomats with very cold feet.

Why two harmless California parents looked suspect we didn't know, but at such times, in such places, everyone seemed to look questionable—especially if they happened to be American.

The first question put to us by our interrogator was, "Why does your American President keep spending money on armaments, forcing us to do the same, thereby taking milk from our babies?" From there, he launched into a tirade over our country being responsible for the downing of the Korean passenger plane. Just having heard the news ourselves, we were ill-equipped to respond.

Even had we been thoroughly informed, how could a couple of ordinary guys deal with this when we were up against such pros? Finally Rudy responded with what I felt was a guaranteed one-way ticket to Siberia. "Well," he said, "we know our country is not always right, but yours may not be always right, either. Isn't this true?"

A longer pause ensued—a bad comedian's angst while waiting for laughs. I felt like Mary Poppins sent to deal with the KGB. In a voice of mock bravado, I followed Rudy's statement with, "We aren't responsible for the plane incident or all that our President does. We are just trying to bring about a little good for no money, without political or religious connections."

"What do you hope to accomplish with your children's art?" they asked. "Who pays you?"

"We pay our own way" was Rudy's answer.

In desperation, I followed up with, "I believe the world needs help and lighting one candle is better than cursing the darkness."

A new thought in these circles. The interpreter was instructed to make a note of it. When I explained that many Americans do what they believe in for no money, our interrogators again looked skeptical. At this point, I was obviously reaching for anything when I said, "Do you know the American expression, 'Give us a break'?" This brought a smile to the face of the man with the U.S. accent. It looked like a million bucks to Rudy and me.

The ice had definitely started to melt. "Do you think it's not worth trying to get through a crack in a wall using means not yet tried?" I asked. The man's smile continued to give me the courage that I thought was long gone.

As we moved to another not quite so ominous-looking room, we noticed a pile of children's art. It was not discussed. A samovar with cookies arrived and we "broke cookies" together. Something changed for the better, and we didn't care what it was. Things were definitely looking up. We gave them the 25 American paintings we had brought, which consisted of a mix of young children's finger paintings and a junior high school's paintings of rock stars. If they were shocked, their expressions showed no sign of it.

Somewhat reluctantly, the interrogator went to a closet and came out with 25 pieces of beautiful student art depicting the old city of Riga with its cobbled streets and buildings with tiled peaked roofs, along with scenes of their Baltic Sea. We thanked them profusely.

We sighed, feeling this would be our last meeting, which, I must admit, left me less than tearful. Arriving back at our hotel, we were totally surprised to receive a message saying we would be picked up in an hour and taken to our interrogator's son's school. Rudy had the feeling that, by now, they had checked with headquarters and decided we were harmless.

"But we told them that," I said, trying to inject a light note into a heavy experience.

Arriving at our first Latvian school, I received a rib-crunching hug from a large-framed art teacher when she learned that I, too, was an art instructor. We gave what art we had left to excited students. Walking back to our waiting black funereal-looking limousine, I said laughing to Rudy, "Looks like they gave us a break after all."

Since this second USSR visit, we have sent to and received art from three Soviet schools. We treasure this alliance. One of our local girls continually corresponds with a young ballerina like herself in Kiev as a result of her Paintbrush Diplomacy connection.

Ever since our brush with the KGB, art has continued to flow between our American students and those of Latvia. We tell ourselves, as our grandchildren play store with our unredeemable Russian rubles, "The price was right."

ESTONIA REVISITED

Estonia—1984

Classroom in Estonia

Before taking off for Eastern Europe, we had a two-day layover in New York. Quite by accident, our hotel room overlooked a huge media event.

Presidents from around the world were attending a children's summit dealing with the feeding and clothing of street children. Watching the richly dressed dignitaries arrive and leave in their long, shimmering limos created a sharp contrast for us when we arrived in Estonia.

Estonia, one of the Baltic states along with Latvia and Lithuania, is the most northern of the three countries and the coldest when winter arrives. We sun-drenched Californians approached it with respect, coats, mufflers, and a lively step. After passing through the dimly lit lobby of what was considered Tallinn's "best" hotel, we arrived in our room, where ever optimistic Rudy surprised me as he assessed the scene from our fourth floor window.

"This place must have been George Orwell's inspiration to write *1984*," he remarked.

My impression as an artist needed just one word. "Gray," I said, looking at colorless bodies moving toward buses and street corners, carrying weather-beaten umbrellas. Women all wore wool hats pulled well over their ears. Our room, however, was so overheated that we opened the window to a bracing icy wind off the Baltic Sea. "Don't complain," I said. The people below would probably quite gladly trade with us."

Most Americans, ourselves included, thought areas like these would soon join the rest of free Eastern Europe. We discovered early the fallacy of our often too simplistic U.S. way of thinking. The Soviet Union still had a firm hold on the Baltic states, and Tallinn Estonians were well aware of this. From what we saw, their better times were a long way off. After work, one of the joys for the people seemed to be patiently lining up in the cold rain, awaiting the opening of the one department store across from our hotel. The queues looked like they would never end, and one night we decided to see what the great attraction was. Inside we saw people milling about in a very disorganized manner, often confronted by empty departments. Where merchandise did exist, it was of such poor quality that it was sad to imagine how long their purchase would last. Probably longer than their near worthless rubles, we surmised.

Although we had brought our international student art exchange program around the world for the past 12 years, we began feeling our art almost too superficial an offering in this poor area.

Because we had a contact with the cultural director of Tallinn, we picked up our world-traveled, worse-for-wear art portfolio and waved down one of the few available cabs. Struggling with much sign language and undergoing a frustrating exchange, we finally meet with Toomie, our contact. He actually remembered us from our first visit to Tallinn in 1983. At that time, the communist regime put on a good front, and the KGB even put us on their 6:00 p.m. TV news program. Now rumor had it the Russians were coming to the border of little Estonia for bread.

"I'll believe anything now," we said, almost in unison.

Our escort arranged for us to meet with some junior-high-school girls. They were talented, pretty, and spoke excellent English. Since the winding down of Russian influence, we were told, English was the new compulsory second language.

Handing them our U.S. students' art gifts brought a response of such joy that any feeling of bringing cake when they needed bread soon vanished. A touch of America seemed to have the effect of a magic mental vitamin pill. They gave us unique Estonian student art and walked us back to our hotel, letting friends along the way know we were from America.

"You must continue your art in the future, you're so talented," I told one of the girls.

"There is no way here," she said, "and we cannot get out." She went on to explain that the Russian government did not openly refuse exit to other countries, but "Red tape" subtly made for never-ending delays.

Before we left for Poland, Toomie insisted on taking us out to lunch. We tried to pay, but he would have none of it. The restaurant offered food I could not describe. Throughout the meal, served by waiters who served only sporadically, our host asked that we speak softly as security was everywhere. I had no appetite and tried to forgo his insistence on offering us dessert.

"Dessert will be the best of the meal," he said. After a 15-minute wait we were each brought full bowls of whipping cream, completely unaccompanied by fruit or anything else to lessen the guilt.

"Treat," he beamed. We ate, every cholesterol-filled bite, thanking him profusely.

We departed, leaving our remaining rubles to be used in Tallinn's children's museum. We had our treat, however, and it wasn't a bowl of whipping cream but the animated faces of the students receiving our gift of American student art. It was their dessert treat also. "We will stay in touch," we told them.

"If just one young person in Estonia makes one contact in the free world, it was worth the trip," Rudy said as we headed for the airport, fighting the cold and pulling our Estonian wool hats over our tender American ears.

BEHIND THE IRON CURTAIN—
WE LEAVE THE FREE WORLD

Berlin, Dresden, Warsaw, Krakow—1984

Checkpoint Charlie

Our master plan for travel had generally gone something like this: "Let's take on the difficult countries before we get too decrepit, and ease into the more conventional routes with whatever we have left." The Eastern European countries might have been less difficult for us 10 years before we took them on, but we were too caught up in our quest to know it. "Anyone can be an observer of people in St. Mark's Square in Venice," Rudy reminded me.

"Eastern Europe is where the need is," my crusader instincts responded. Little did we realize what a bonus freedom was.

In 1984 we entered West Berlin, thus giving us a better idea of what freedom versus communism was really about. The West Berliners had quite an opulent world on their side of the communist Wall, making me think of the extremes freedom or restriction could bring. Uninhibited graffiti told it all.

During a short stay here, our U.S. Mission driver gave us a very informative tour. He explained the division of Germany after World War II, when the U.S., British, and French zones of occupation were reconstituted as West Germany, and the Soviet zone of occupation became East Germany. West Berlin was part of the former while East Berlin was the capital of the latter. The Berlin Wall was erected in 1961.

This tour provided our last look at the free world. The next day we would cross over into East Germany.

The U.S. Mission driver picked us up in the morning, drove us to within a block of the Berlin Wall, and left us. He told us this would avoid any suspicion that we might be collaborating with anyone in the West. We were flattered that we might be considered for this James Bond role.

Walking, we approached Checkpoint Charlie, once again looking like pack mules with all of our equipment. The children's art portfolio seemed always to take the longest to inspect because it evoked the greatest measure of suspicion. As we looked at the appliance-white eastern side of the Berlin Wall, we realized we were in a whole different "ballpark." The game was over—the guards, gates, checkpoints, and police dogs high above in watchtowers made this all too plain. (Thank you, California Congressman Tom Lantos, for giving us government approval. We needed fortifying about now!)

Because of a lack of public transportation (no taxis or buses were in sight), we set out on foot for our U.S. embassy. Struggling along with backpacks, portfolio, and suitcases, we were a show-stopper. Somber-faced observers appeared from every direction. Resting each block and putting my suitcase down for a breather made the sight of the waving American flag in the distance look like manna from heaven. We could almost feel our hearts beating out the rhythm of "The Star-Spangled Banner."

After meeting with our embassy people we took a three-hour train ride south to Dresden, Rudy's birthplace. On arrival we met with Paul Arnold, a friend we had known since the Dresden art exhibit in San Francisco. Paul took us to his home where we met his wife and two sons, who were still living on the stories and pictures he had brought back from his stay in San Francisco. It was a somewhat sad encounter, since they realized they would never again be able to visit such a place or have their own car in their lifetime. The saddest for the parents was the fact that their sons were unable to enter a school of their choice because of their religious background. Religion of any sort was penalized and discriminated against.

We had brought the boys silver American Indian belt buckles, a small offering under the circumstances. They were so overcome with joy that the younger boy insisted on wearing his to bed. We discovered American Indian items were very big here and wished we had brought more—famous last words, these!

Bright and early the next morning, a communist representative met us with his little black car. After a tour of Dresden's beautiful cultural center, the Zwinger, we were brought to several "children's palaces," once true palaces, now serving to encourage children who are especially gifted in the arts.

How impressed we were with the serious time given to children's art, and how we wished the same attention were given to art in many of our own public schools!

The art we received from these students included some of my favorites in our entire Paintbrush collection. Obviously the Berlin Wall had not stopped the flow of the children's creative juices. Each child also gave us his or her lesson in Roman lettering done that day. It spelled *Frieden* (peace).

When we returned to our driver, his only comment was, "Twenty-five pairs of eyes saw and heard two Americans trying to spread peace in their own way. Children know what you are about, and they will remember."

Moved by this whole experience, I am sure it was even more emotional for Rudy, who might have gone to that school had his parents not brought him to the free world. Rudy doesn't show too much open emotion, but I know he hoped he had brought the best of both cultures together in some small way.

Despite the somewhat wrenching farewell experience with the Arnold family,

India Age 7

India Age 12

Ireland Age 14

Ireland Age 11

Northern Ireland Age 10

Northern Ireland Age 11

Narthern Ireland Age 13

Ireland Age 12

Northern Ireland Age 14

whom we would probably never see again, our thoughts had to be on our next destination—Poland.

We were told to arrange for a cab the night before to take us to the station for our train trip from Dresden to Warsaw. At 7:15 a.m. we were waiting outside our hotel, as was our driver with a cab that was somewhat *kaput* (German slang for not functioning up to standard). Thank goodness for German mechanical expertise; we made our train without the near coronary experiences we have sometimes had.

Our 13-hour train ride east to Warsaw proved to be one more meaningful experience. A movie buff, I felt it great material for a short cinema presentation. Rudy moved right into a German conversation with another native of Dresden, on his way to visit his Polish relatives. (At every opportunity, Rudy practiced his German. I was everlastingly grateful, as it had pulled us out of many a tight squeak.)

Come lunchtime, Rudy's new acquaintance broke open a gourmet delight, prepared by his German wife, which could have fed an army. He insisted on sharing it. I was glad our original polite refusal was not taken seriously, as nothing else proved to be available.

Doors kept opening and closing, as different people entered our compartment. A very pregnant young Polish girl entered with a beautiful blue-eyed, rosy-cheeked baby. She was going to Warsaw to be checked for the possibility of twins this time.

At the next stop, a young woman with a baby entered and threw her baby on the lap of a young stranger, while she adjusted her paraphernalia in the overhead rack. It seemed she had enough to last her and the baby for at least a month, certainly more than we had between the two of us for a similar time. The young man accepted the baby with complete naturalness, even popping its pacifier in its mouth, and patiently waited for the young mother to reclaim her child.

From then on, all of us seemed to become a family. Language was no barrier. The young temporary baby sitter turned out to be an English teacher; the German-speaking Dresden man and Rudy filled in when necessary; and the Polish women shared thoughts with me on "baby land."

Once more the never-empty picnic basket emerged and we all had more smoked duck. Rudy and I contributed chocolate bars. Hesitantly, we offered a Michael Jackson pin to the young teacher, and he pinned it on his chest as if we had presented him with the merit honor of the year.

This whole encounter made our train ride seem like it had hardly begun, now that it was about to draw to a close.

Looking at the English teacher, we asked that he offer our fellow passengers a parting message. "Tell them all we hate to leave people who made us feel like part of a family." Kissing the babies, we headed for our next destination, but not before we dug into our backpack for one more Michael Jackson pin, hesitantly requested by the young teacher for a good friend.

We arrived in Warsaw, Poland, with no taxi available and bus conveyances jammed. You might think we would be used to this scene by now. Unable to speak Polish and struggling to get to our hotel with all our gear amid crowds of people pushing from all sides, I was close to a feeling of desperation.

Out of the crowd, a young student suddenly emerged, handed me his books, and taking my gear, led us to our hotel. I threw my arms around him and gave my best embrace, though my energy level was near zero.

The next day our embassy people met us at our hotel and set us up with an interpreter and a school for the next day. A good night's sleep was in order— usually fortifying us for the next day when we would be off and running. I often wonder what keeps us going at such times, but I don't have time to ponder.

At eight in the morning, a young TV woman and her husband arrived to take us to a children's art center. They apologized for having their car trunk full of the newspapers they would exchange for toilet paper. "We will put your children's art on the top of these," they explained apologetically. There was much poverty here, and lines for items most easily obtained in the States were a reality everywhere.

Bronislawa and her composer-husband brought us to a children's center, where I saw the most original children's art so far. Papier-mâché likenesses depicting figures from their bad dreams were made by the children, with the idea that, through art, the children could get rid of their demons. Animals were made from such vegetables as small potatoes, which looked like mice when the children added pins for eyes and string for tails. These children artists and I were soul mates!

The next day, outside of a Catholic Church service, we met a young priest to whom we gave our last $50 for baby clothes, which we had heard were hard to come by. "We have plenty of travelers' checks to carry us till our next stop," Rudy assured me in his innocence.

A side trip to Krakow was well worth our time. We were introduced to Bronia (a popular name), a Polish woman working in our U.S. consulate. She took us on a wonderful tour of this historic city, including a number of schools where we once more exchanged and received marvelous art.

We also visited a hospital donated by the United States called the City of Hope Hospital. We had thought our country was responsible only for the City of Hope Hospital Ship. This was gratifying news as so much need existed there. We met with terminally ill children, anxiously awaiting us with their touching crayon drawings.

When we presented them with our students' work, the nurses put it up all around the walls. The children reacted with such joy, each wearing a little flowered hospital gown, but even their smiles and laughter could not stop my eyes from overflowing. In moments like these, our expenses, doubts, and struggles could not quench our desire to continue with Paintbrush Diplomacy. Parting was doubly hard this time. A young woman, carefully looking around to be sure she wasn't observed, gave us a solidarity sign as she smiled and turned the corner. We sincerely felt these people were unbeatable.

RUDE AWAKENING

Krakow Train to Budapest—1984

City of Hope Hospital in Krakow

Boarding a train in Krakow, Poland, for a speaking appointment in Budapest, Hungary, my husband Rudy and I were the epitome of two innocent Americans. We were looking forward to a restful journey and, although this was then communist territory, we felt that any difficulties we might encounter could be set right by a wire or phone call to our loyal California congressman.

"Traveling 13-hours by train will make us feel closer to the earth and the Polish people," we told each other as we dragged our luggage over cobbled streets to the depot. The local people were entertained by our wheeled luggage and amused when mine caught in cracks, nearly toppling over. We smiled with them. Told by our embassy people that locals booked their train rides far in advance, we were grateful to them for securing us the last available second-class compartment.

Only as we started climbing the train stairs did our feelings of euphoria begin to drift away. The admonition of our older son, Paul, returned to me, "Now don't you guys act so trusting in those countries! We can't help you there." Already it was too late!

The platform below the train steps was such a distance from the train that I could make the first step only with extreme effort. I pulled my luggage up, stretching my short legs as Rudy pulled the heaviest suitcase and our large art portfolio. A kindly looking workman lifted me up the last step—a much-needed boost.

Peasant women, with their belongings wrapped in heavy colored sackcloth, banged into us as they tried to get a place in unassigned seats. We became part of the struggle. Fortunately, a birdcage with a chirping bird did not go into our compartment. Children clung to mother's legs, and the smell of food wrapped for sustenance on the long journey permeated the air.

After much pushing and pulling, we finally arrived in our tiny compartment for six passengers and were handed two cardboardlike sheets for our cot-sized beds. Climbing over bags and excited Polish travelers, we tried to release the folded cots from the wall, but to no avail.

My husband's German was no help in breaking the communication gap. We were packed in like sardines, and the aroma of bodies, baked ham, onions, and garlic was second only to cigarette smoke, which almost defied visibility. Finally, after slipping a couple of dollars to a Polish train employee wearing a long white apron, our sleeping accommodations were made as comfortable as possible. Fortunately, we removed only our shoes for the trip. Although it was neither lunch time nor dinner time, people insisted on sharing their food with us. Passengers sat in upper bunks dangling their legs, using beds as couches. A generous man across from us insisted we share his whole roast chicken. It was delicious.

When darkness descended, Rudy and I decided we should try for sleep. We wanted to keep our Budapest appointment with a semblance of consciousness. I climbed into my cot and turned to the wall, hoping to find a pocket of air that was less smoke-filled. Six Poles conversing, smoking, and talking all night did not make sleep a great possibility, but insomnia seemed a small hardship compared to lung cancer. Rudy's snoring was not discernible over the growing festive mood of the Poles. They probably had few places to congregate without the listening ear of Big Brother. Our compartment was fast becoming a raucous social club.

Only a few hours into sleep, we were shocked into semiconsciousness by a sudden banging on the compartment door. Instant silence, followed by armed border guards entering our compartment!

"So what," I said under my breath, "we're Americans bringing goodwill. This isn't Jane Fonda in a movie concealing spy information in her hat. We have nothing to fear." All the movies I had ever seen of such encounters became pale by comparison with being personally confronted by this situation. Rudy, still in the arms of Morpheus, was brought up short with a firm billy club crack on his feet.

As the guards entered the compartment, the Poles assumed a docile attitude, in direct contrast to their previous festive loquaciousness. Only when the officers came to us did the compartment resemble the child's game Statues. The atmosphere made a shocking transition from camaraderie to a deathlike sobriety. No one moved a muscle except Rudy and me who, half awake, fumbled through our luggage for our passports. After handing them over we were asked for $24, the fee for cutting across a small section of what was then Czechoslovakia. Rudy said, "We didn't even put our feet on the earth there."

At that point we were still thinking we had American rights, but when one of the officers' rifles brushed my shoulder, I was amazed at how quickly I grasped the rigidity of what we were up against. There was no reasoning, by hand language or otherwise; $24 was what they wanted and we didn't have it. Polish money or travelers' checks wouldn't do. We had no U.S. dollars, having expected to get to a bank in Budapest.

"Problem, problem," the soldiers kept repeating (in an accent that defies my typewriter), pointing to the train tracks. I couldn't believe they meant what I thought they seemed to mean. We would have to get off the train in what appeared to be the middle of a totally uninhabited forest, in the black of night, in pouring rain. Rudy brought out what we thought was an impressive-looking letter from our congressman, with a gold seal in one corner, validating our children's art exchange program. They looked about as impressed as if he had handed them a pass to the county fair.

As a last appeal I even offered the only thing I had left, my thin gold wedding band. Sentiment can become too great a luxury when a situation has no options. It was to no avail. It was refused, and we were quickly putting on our shoes and gathering our luggage. Out we went, accompanied by our military escorts. Every eye was upon these two American passengers as we dragged our luggage down the stairs and left the train. The silence was palpable—it seemed to fill the air. Passing the train compartment we had shared with our Polish friends, I saw the face of the generous man who had shared his roast chicken. Looking down at us, he raised two fingers in a V for victory signal. I felt stronger.

As I descended the train steps and started walking the wet tracks with the military on either side of me, I mustered all the pioneer stock I could, straightened my shoulders, and marched. When frightened enough, I often rally my forces and am at my best, but a small voice whispered, "We may never see our children again." To that voice I replied, "I'll be darned if I let these two tin soldiers see an American woman cry!" One looked no older than our 19-year-old son, John.

As I walked the wet train tracks, carrying a suitcase with the military at my side, my sandal slipped, and I did come close to crying. Rudy was walking the tracks behind me, carrying his suitcase and the portfolio of art. The walk seemed interminable. We figured it to be about three miles, but it felt like 30. We walked the tracks with our armed escorts until another train came along, heading back to where we started seven hours ago.

Finally the soldier on my right took my suitcase and we were directed aboard the train. As he placed my belongings on the train platform, Rudy exclaimed, "My God, they're going to send us all the way back to Krakow!"

Wet, cold, and sleepless, we got in an unheated train and stretched out on the seat. I took Rudy's wool socks from my backpack and wrapped them around his bald head. I found another pair in my bag and put them on my cold feet. I pulled my tam over my ears and we tried to huddle away the cold until a conductor cracked our feet off the seat with his club, and we gave up on sleep.

Trying to breathe a note of levity into a pretty sad situation, I offered, "And all that smoke for nothing!" This time Rudy didn't laugh.

BUDAPEST AT LAST

Krakow to Budapest and Yugoslavia—1984

The Marketplace

Once more on the streets of Krakow at 7:00 a.m., we had no recourse but to look up the U.S. consulate. Seeing the Stars and Stripes waving at the entrance to the building made us feel we were coming home once more.

Back at the U.S. consulate, drenched, no hotel, no food, and no sleep, we looked like a couple of old hippies thrown off a train. We were! The consul general took us in with loving kindness—even offering us his room, knowing only too well what tough times were. He was one of the "yellow ribbon" returnees from Lebanon. We, too, needed all the love we could get. This offer was more than tempting, but we had an appointment to keep in Budapest.

Our U.S. people drove us to the airport in Warsaw and we again hugged and thanked them.

We arranged for a plane that would work into our schedule this time. An airplane never looked so good!

Since we had not slept, eaten, or changed clothes in 24 hours, our Budapest hotel looked too fancy for the likes of us. In the lobby we passed a gold-framed mirror. My hair looked like a wet feather fan and Rudy's pants seemed to have gotten smaller. Ah, the resilience of the human being! I understood the feelings of kidnapped victim Patty Hearst as, like her, we had been confined to small areas under surveillance for too long.

As we stood at the desk to get our key, the hotel clerk wasn't sure he was handing the important-looking envelope to the right people. When we got to our room and opened it, we weren't sure either that we were the right people. It was a gold-engraved invitation from our embassy, inviting us to a State Department cocktail party for people in the arts.

"If they could only see us now," Rudy laughed. "Are you game, Char?" he asked, looking at the bedraggled creature beside him.

"Well I've got one decent dress that might rally if I hang it in the shower to get out the worst wrinkles. When my hair dries out fully, maybe I can take a scarf and do something that will transform me into a terribly arty-looking woman and fool everyone. What do you think?"

"Go for it!" he said, showing no sign of doubt (if he felt any). I didn't tell him his suit looked as if it had shrunk.

I tied a beautiful Polish silk scarf around my hair and Rudy shaved off two days of beard. We looked at each other in the lobby mirror and almost wondered who these quite acceptable-looking people were.

The party made our walk on the tracks a distant memory as people around us laughed and talked freely. Trays of familiar-looking American food were offered with never-ending wine refills. Some people actually knew of our program to exchange American students' art and letters with that of their foreign counterparts and praised our efforts. We did not tell them what an effort it sometimes was. It didn't matter now. The dress was no longer wrinkled and the scarf hid a multitude of sins. We had a ball! Ah, what a bath and a few creature comforts can do!

The Hungarian people are much better off than the Polish. The children were able to enjoy special classes outside of regular school—in little country towns where they made art from the scenery and drew the peasants in their ethnic clothing. Many children did beautiful work from inexpensive linoleum blocks, and several prints could be made from a single carved-out drawing. The Impressionists were studied and the children learned the manner in which their mentors created. The teacher had them make their own form of Impressionist art to better understand this type of creative experience. We were given many of their most beautiful woodblock prints, and have since been sent more art and letters. Our students look at them in awe when we pass them around U.S. classrooms as we tell about these young artists and their country.

Our gift of U.S. student art, often depicting the great variation in scenery and culture throughout our large, diversified country, is always received with excitement throughout the world's classrooms. Anything depicting our movie world, cartoons, or rock stars always brings the greatest response. These areas are certainly not all we are about, but other countries envy and emulate the creative, innovative spark that is truly the flavor of America.

We always wish we could stay in each stop longer. But with appointments in Yugoslavia, our final stop, we once more packed our travel-weary clothes, now-bulging art portfolio (we always seem to return with more than the 200 pieces of U.S. art we bring), and got ready for the next exciting adventure.

We left on one more too-early train ride for Yugoslavia, a comparatively uneventful trip, which we needed and relished. Along the way, we nurtured ourselves on the beautiful scenery. Zagreb presented us with quite a different, more affluent, kind of communism than we had seen so far.

Tito, their ruler, who made some very elastic rules for a settlement after the end of World War II, enabled Yugoslavia to put together more of a socialistic kind of communism. To a couple of Californians, the freedom the Yugoslavs were so proud of seemed pretty restrictive, but then our Golden State–type of "laid back" culture sometimes makes us feel that other states in our country are quite conservative. The Yugoslavian people graciously wined and dined us (these people don't believe in snacks). We were given art and a promise of student letters. One English teacher was particularly interested in adding a letter-writing project to her curriculum. I hope our American jargon doesn't throw them off the track.

When I told our grandson Nicholas of this idea of his school connecting with this Yugoslavian school, he lit up and said, "Hey, fresh, Char!" (Translation: "great!")

Eastern Europe was one of our hardest but most meaningful trips. "This one really separated the men from the boys, and the women from the girls," I told Rudy. With *glasnost* and great changes looming on the horizon for the communist world, we are very optimistic. I like to think that we and the new generation had a sort of *glasnost* before the very energetic Mr. Gorbachev appeared on the scene. We only hope that all can join in bringing our young people together so that they can build a world more peaceful than ours. We don't care what name they care to call their peace builder. All we can say is, "Paint it as bright as you can!"

TOO CLOSE FOR COMFORT
WITHOUT FRIENDSHIP

Panama, Ecuador, Peru, Chile, Argentina, Brazil—1985

Riding the Reins

Arriving in Panama to begin our South American trip in 1985, we were hit by steaming air, the U.S. military presence, and an overwhelming sense of pride when we came face to face with the Panama Canal.

Grammar-school geography classes couldn't begin to tell the full story of what our engineers had accomplished. "We Americans have such a capability and inventiveness with which to aid areas like this," I suggested. "That's where our talents should go." No need for response; our travels so often had confirmed these thoughts.

Sometimes our connections with young people and educators in a foreign country open up without much effort, but in this case we had to do some digging. Contacts don't always fall in line and back-up letters get lost. We are no strangers to waiting in school offices while our credentials are checked.

Finally we were brought to our first Panamanian classroom after such a wait, but the atmosphere seemed slightly guarded. "Nice that they worked us into their schedule on such short notice," we tell each other.

We gave the students a short run-down on what Paintbrush Diplomacy is about, the countries we have been to with our program, and what we hoped to accomplish for the world, particularly for their generation. They were polite, but once we opened up our art portfolio and held up our U.S. student art, the ice—or in this case, the steam—was broken. (The oohs and ahs are the same all over the world.) The principal entered just about the time we had caused order to be replaced by pandemonium.

Students were all clustered around the teacher's desk covered by our art gifts. It seemed as if we all suddenly became one. Per usual, Rudy's and my adrenalin kicked in. Addresses were exchanged, art of the students was brought to us, and a Paintbrush Diplomacy link was set up. How short the wait in the office seemed by the time we waved goodbye and, once more, shy students followed us to the door.

Our second Panamanian school was an Episcopalian Spanish-English one, the work of a former U.S. diplomat. An enthusiastic principal, who had all of her classes speaking both languages, was anxious for the students to become involved in a global education program. We were an answer to her prayers. She could give us no art on this short notice but promised to send us as much as we left.

We always prefer to make a two-way exchange right then so that our children at home don't go wanting or become discouraged by what sometimes amounts to a long wait. This verbal agreement, however, proved to be as good as the principal's promise. A firm commitment began and has continued.

Our next day began with an early flight to Quito, Ecuador. (By early I mean 3:00 a.m.!) We landed at 7:00 a.m. at an 8,000-foot altitude, which could have taken a greater toll on me were it not for a caring New York doctor who had supplied me with a couple of fluid pills.

Another much-welcomed kindness came from our Congressman Tom Lantos' office explaining our needs. As a result our embassy took care of a number of school meetings, in spite of the fact that we were misinformed about their school schedules. Regular sessions were on vacation, but we were taken to delightful summer schools. This unexpected development was extremely rewarding, as art was their only priority.

Entering a classroom from the pouring rain, we were soon warm when little schoolchildren sat on our laps. Others made beautiful collage art from old magazines and colored tissue paper. They went into raptures when we gave them our young students' paintings of Snoopy or Mickey Mouse. Older students, learning our home was San Francisco, asked if we were on the TV program "The Streets of San Francisco." We always tried to straighten them out by explaining how ordinary and hard-working most Americans are. Some almost looked a little disappointed, wanting to think that we all live in a sort of magic never-never land—that the streets here are truly paved with gold.

The following morning our embassy presented us with a delightful surprise in the form of a young Ecuadorian woman, an archaeology student studying the restoration of religious artifacts. Our new guide warned that embassies were no longer safe havens for people like us. Barricades were everywhere; rope ladders hung from windows. Just the week before, the embassy had received another of its many bomb threats. Sobering words these, but obviously not enough to stop us.

On our first outing with our interesting new accomplice, Rudy was hustled against a revolving door while leaving the Cathedral of San Francisco. Looking up the hill at a departing group of natives, he exclaimed, "There they go!"

Patting his pocket, he realized he was lighter by the weight of his wallet and all it contained. A jacket full of zippered pockets that I had bought for both of us for safety reasons was obviously no deterrent. Fortunately, the embassy people lent us enough to get by until our arrival in Peru where, true to the company's advertising, our charge card was replaced the next day. (Poverty is so rampant that even casually dressed travelers are bait.)

Our next stop in Quito was a real experience and showed us the flavor of Indian life that was all too quickly becoming immersed in the outside world. Women wearing back derby hats came in from the countryside each morning with babies, wrapped in beautiful hand-woven blankets, hanging from their backs. They carried their wares to the market on their heads. I hated to see the industrialized world changing their mountain lifestyle. With some sadness I told Rudy, "Their babies will probably wind up sorting microchips in a computer factory when they grow up."

To comfort me he answered, "Or they will be showing us gringos how to copy the beautiful earthen dyes in their weavings with synthetic replicas."

"That doesn't make me feel that much better," I told him.

On our last day in Quito, our lovely guide, interpreter, and moneylender took us to another summer art school where children offered us their handmade puppets, which were hanging from classroom ceilings. Our portfolio would not allow for this, but the temptation to have the delightful little figures sent through diplomatic pouch by our embassy was strong. Rudy became too honorable, saying, "No, Char, we're lucky to have these good people supplying us with an interpreter, guide, and caretaker." I felt like a deprived child, but acquiesced.

Back we went to an early dinner (better call it lunch in these parts) and a much needed rest, as we would depart the next day for a 5:00 a.m. flight to Lima, Peru.

When I have miscalculated the weather, I have often been known to tie a heavy clothing item in a knot and throw it under a bed so that a worker (usually in a Moslem or communist country) will not return it. I am always trying to make more room when I see something I simply can't resist for our grandchildren. Fortunately in this case, I hadn't thrown out my thermal underwear before we headed for the highest areas of the Andes. I loved the llamas even more when I wrapped a llama scarf around my head and ears. "Welcome as a lover's kiss," I told Rudy.

"It's *not* that cold!" said overoptimistic Rudy with a blue nose. When he got a little bluer, I fixed him up with a llama hat. He loved it.

The next morning two women from the Peruvian Cultural Center met us in our hotel lobby, telling us they would bring us their student art the following Thursday. Lucy Alvarez and her interpreter pal told us they had lined up more contacts than we could get to. Sometimes the places we have little contact with beforehand turn out to be the most productive upon our arrival. Always an adventure one way or another.

By evening both Rudy's and my body further yielded to the cold, so we bought lovely alpaca sweaters from a native Peruvian Indian woman. That afternoon we treated ourselves to a city tour, winding up with a young American couple from Arizona. The woman asked to sit with me on the bus, as she was lonely for home.

Her husband was here on business for his pharmaceutical company. Her stories of the recent kidnappings of American businessmen in the area, along with rumors of Peru being the next country to fall to the communists, didn't exactly buoy up my spirits. Camouflage-suited military guards stood outside our hotel entrance, money-changers were at every corner, and I was warned to remove any gold jewelry before entering a church.

This was only the beginning!

While having a predinner glass of wine in our room, we received a phone call from the hotel office telling Rudy a woman he had given a traveler's check to that afternoon was in the lobby wishing to speak to him. "Apparently she didn't know how to deal with a traveler's check," Rudy explained. "I'll just take a quick run down to the lobby and straighten her our. Keep the wine cold and I'll be back in a minute."

Little did I know what a long minute that would be! As the minutes ticked away, my imagination drifted back to my afternoon conversation on the bus with the young woman from Arizona. Rudy had taken our only room key with him, and although there was a guard on every floor, I didn't like leaving our room unlocked to go down to the lobby in search of Rudy. Calls to the desk clerk brought no satisfactory answers, so I finally went down to see what was going on. No sign of anyone but the clerk and a few bellboys who acted stunned by my frantic, "Donde está mi esposo?" question, or my exclamation, "Vamos, Señor Pribuss! Desperado!" I said, throwing up my hands. All attention was, of course, focused on this crazy American woman.

Finally, after half an hour that seemed like a lifetime, Rudy and the Peruvian saleswoman who had sold us our sweaters appeared in the entrance of the hotel. I ran to Rudy, threw my arms around him, and cried. He had gone to a money-changer with the señora to get her the true worth of our traveler's check. Apparently she was getting cheated at the bank, and her livelihood was so close to the edge that she too was "desperado." Her womanly instincts joined with mine as she threw her arms around me, giving me an embrace that almost made up for it all.

Returning somewhat back to normal, I made Rudy swear that we would never be parted when out of the country. Being completely on our own, rather than in a tour group, makes two a lot safer than one. I didn't know whether to hug him again or beat him. "Which woman do you care about more?" I demanded. "You hardly knew *her!*"

To this day, he swears he had no idea I would be so upset. With all the running around they had to do, the time just flew. Men are so different…

The next morning, another 5:00 a.m. departure—but this time by train. We were going to what some call the "top of the world" to see the ruins of Machu Picchu. The train ride through the first rain forest I had been in reminded me of "The Little Train That Could," a story I had read so often to our children. Puffing along with the sound of Peruvian flute music accompanying the clickity-clack of the train's wheels put us in a sort of enchanted state.

The bus that met us, taking us to what truly did seem like the top of the world, was a runner-up to a Harrison Ford adventure movie. Rudy's favorite expression worked in nicely about now, "Well, Char, as we say, it beats the nursing home."

As is the case with so many harrowing rides, all is forgotten when the new sight awaits us. This one was particularly awe-inspiring. The precision of the stone structures of these Incan people would have put to shame some of the work done by modern man. Each stone, cut in rectangles, needed no mortar to hold it together, as the fit was so perfect.

This ancient city, built on a mountain more than 6,750 feet high, gave us a feeling of having left the real world behind because of the chiffonlike clouds encircling the very tops of the mountains. People who are affected by altitude should come prepared with proper medication. I was forced to view all of this loveliness from a horizontal position as my gift of fluid pills had run out.

The forced quiet of this temporary setback allowed me to meditate quietly on the detachment I felt in this amazing place, but I wouldn't recommend it if prevention is available.

Children in the city of Cuzco, 50 miles northwest of Machu Picchu, had a brief visit with us before our trip to the mountain. They wanted us to pick up their artwork on our stopover back to Lima. The teacher said he would conduct a contest in our absence. We were amazed at the great desire of the South American children and educators to form a connection with the students and educators of North America.

The art gifts of the Cuzco children were wonderful, often depicting their culture and family life. The art professor and his little daughter even awaited us at the airport for our flight (another early one!) back to Lima. He felt he had a need for art textbooks to better teach his students. I promised to send some but wished we could have brought *him* to some of our U.S. art classes, just the way he was. The art of his students certainly showed he was doing something very right.

Once more back in Lima, we met with art teachers and government people who had been so kind to us. We decided to give all of them a little thank-you party in our hotel, which most of them had never been in—and probably never would be in again. Tea, Coca-Cola, and cookies caused a response of such joy that we were almost as thrilled as they were. When we settled up our hotel bill, the desk clerk questioned the consumption by Rudy and me of 50 Cokes between us!

Our next bus to the airport would mean a 2:00 a.m. rising, so I was long into sleep when awakened by a phone call at 8:00 p.m. from a little Peruvian girl who had been at our party. She wanted to say one last goodbye. Even though I was only half awake, this little voice would be one I would never forget.

"Hello," she said, "I just want to say goodbye and tell you I love you." What's sleep when you can have a phone call like that?

Our next destination was Chile and, although I looked forward to our stop there, it was hard to think that it could offer more than we had seen so far. Santiago reminded me of Vivian Leigh in *A Streetcar Named Desire*—a once beautiful flower that had lost some of its bloom.

From the '30s to World War II, nitrate was mined here and shipped to all parts of the world. After chemical fertilizers replaced it, a deflated economy followed. The European flavor had a fascination for us, however, but we also felt sadness reflected in the people. Their discontent with their ruler, President Pinochet, who promised to quit but never did, apparently didn't help matters, to put it kindly.

Our embassy arranged for us to visit a boy's Catholic school where Father John was ready and well prepared for our visit. The priest's stories of deprivation in this poor neighborhood were heartbreaking. One of Father John's requests amused us, however.

"You live near Clint Eastwood in Carmel, California. If you could just send us his picture, the boys would love it." We had the feeling that he thought we were intimate friends with Clint.

After a meager repast with the priest, leaving our art gift with his boys, we took off for Argentina.

Now heading toward the last two stops of our South American trip, we were starting to feel a little worse for wear. Packing the last of our 200 pieces of U.S. art in our hotel room (we couldn't have operated without their laundry bags), we got ready for an Argentinian high school.

These students were doing such sophisticated art that we were sorry to have only a few pieces of U.S. art at their age level. (Connecting a grade with the same grade in our country is sometimes hard to do, as we are never quite sure which level of school will be receiving us.) The art we had of rock stars, however, made up for a lot. The students got so excited that their teacher made some wild-sounding Spanish demands to bring back a measure of order.

"Don't you wish our students who gave us this art could see this response?" Rudy asked. How often we have thought this.

"Even better would be for them to bring their own art gifts to foreign students instead of two travel-weary people doing the delivering," I answered.

"They didn't have the dream, though," Rudy said encouragingly. Toward the last leg of a trip, such uppers were always gratefully received.

The next morning we left for Rio de Janeiro, Brazil, with me pretending that Rudy and I were Fred Astaire and Ginger Rogers in the movie *Flying Down to Rio*. Takes a lot of pretending, but I did it. We had run hard, and a little fantasy helped me get the last burst of energy needed.

Arriving at our hotel, we were presented with a packet of "dos and don'ts" by our faithful embassy people:

No cameras at the beaches for security reasons. (Poor Rudy, with all those scantily-clad bathing girls on the beach of Ipanema!)

Don't bathe in the beautiful-looking water because of pollution.

Lock passports in hotel safe.

Staying out after hours could be risky.

Our embassy friends also stipulated a time for us to meet with an interpreter the next morning and be taken to a school. My Spanish was coming along pretty well by now, but mostly Portuguese was spoken here. Good try, Char!

The school we visited was in a rural area, and we talked in a fourth-grade classroom with a dirt floor. However, this took nothing away from the orderliness

Italy Age 13

Italy Age 14

Jamaica Age 11

Jamaica Age 12

Jamaica Age 12

Jamaica Age 11

Japan Age 11

Japan Age 13

Japan Age 10

Latvia Age 11

Latvia Age 13

Latvia Age 13

Lithunia Age 13

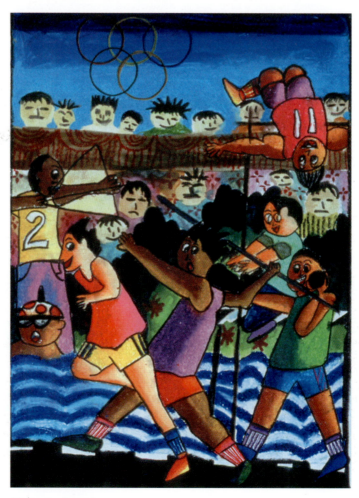

Malaysia Age 11

Mexico Age 9

Mexico Age 10

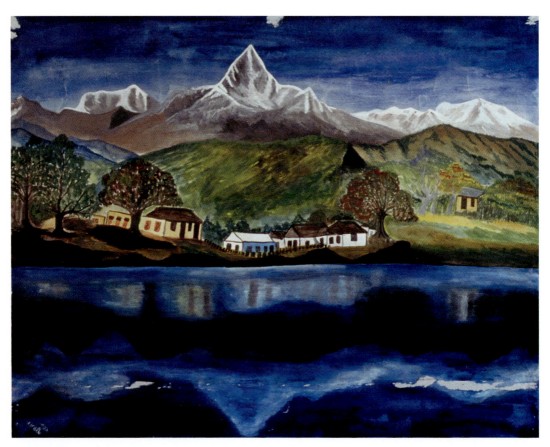

Nepal Age 15

Nepal Age 13

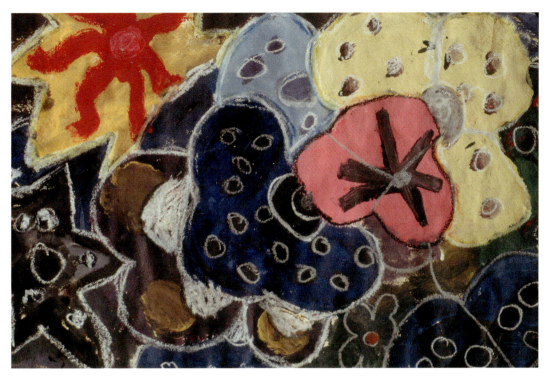

New Zealand Age 8

New Zealand Age 8

New Zealand Age 5

Norway Age 11

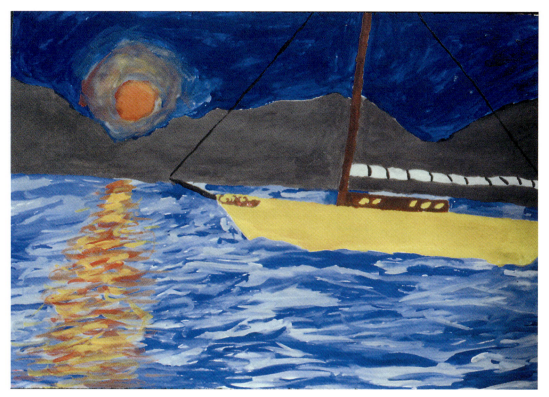

Norway Age 11

Norway Age 14

Oman Age 11

Oman Age 11

Oman Age 10

Panama Age 3

Panama Age 12

Panama Age 13

Panama Age 9

Papa New Guinea Age 10

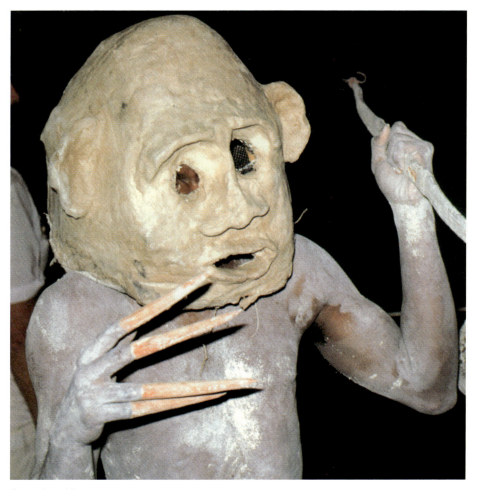

Peru Age 15

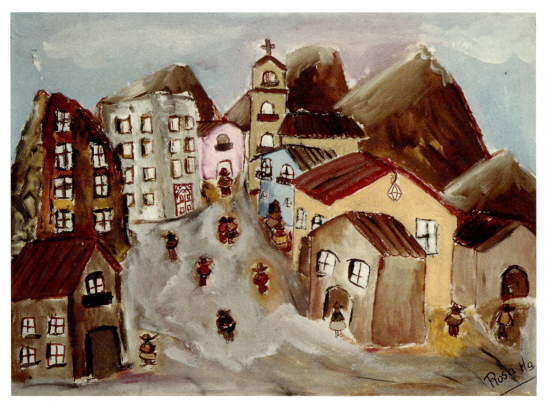

Peru Age 12

Peru Age 12

of things. The mothers had just finished a Brazilian-type P.T.A. meeting when we arrived. Through our interpreter, the mothers and I traded motherly stories. In no time, we were connected by a bond only mothers can relate to.

Before we left, we asked our embassy to set up an art contest for the students with a $50 prize for each of two winners. This idea seemed overwhelming to both our government people and the educators. They explained that this amount of money would be a year's salary for some of the people here.

When we left, there were not just hugs this time but also tears. A year later, our government office sent a marvelous picture of two beaming Brazilian art contest winners receiving our checks. We relived our entire experience while looking at the picture.

Packing what I hadn't thrown under the bed (except for a couple of decent outfits, I bring a lot of "Goodwill" clothes), we thought of home once more. In not quite a month, we had lived a lifetime with people in a continent we never knew before.

When we arrived home, we desperately wanted to impress our government representatives, educators, and children with the need to reach out to our neighbors to the south. Often South American students feel very estranged from ours. Involvement of U.S. citizens here, in government or otherwise, often seemed wanting where the needs were greatest. Unfortunately, we have waited five years to see some real response to our Paintbrush Diplomacy efforts in 1985.

In 1990 the Smithsonian Institution will have a joint venture with us in the form of a traveling student art show from our North and South American collection. "Students of the Americas" will be offered a program where all can become better acquainted through Paintbrush Diplomacy. This exhibit will be a quincentennial celebration of Columbus' landing in the New World.

WHAT A JOY TO COMMUNICATE IN ENGLISH—SORT OF

Irish Republic, Northern Ireland, Wales, Scotland—1986

Ireland

This was our second trip to Ireland. (Our first was before Paintbrush Diplomacy officially began.) Rudy and I were not just a twosome this time. A television educational station released its Girl Friday, Sharon Hancock, to us as a volunteer, and carrying all her heavy equipment, we made a very novice TV group.

Sometimes our connections helped us slide into a culture as easily as silk. Sometimes the entry was more like burlap. Of all places, Dublin was a little tough this time. The U.S. embassy person we anticipated meeting was called to Washington, D.C., the day we arrived, but a little blarney acquired from my Irish grandmother's genes helped pave the way. Connections were set up for us in two schools in Dublin. In each case they soon made us forget our temporary inconveniences. All the children wore uniforms (of course, the boys were in neckties), but the devilment still showed in their sparkling blue eyes. Seeing a painting done by a pretty blonde Argentinian girl whose photo was attached to her art, one young student at the second school poked his neighbor and winked, saying, "Not bad, eh Patrick? I thought those people didn't have girls as pretty as our Colleens."

"I could have told them that girls are girls," Rudy laughed as we got back into the car on our way to Northern Ireland.

After passing through a town with boarded-up windows and blown-up cars, we entered a classroom wallpapered with children's paintings. The contrast of anger built up by adults and the joy of children depicted in clown paintings (a carnival had just visited their town) was almost more than we could adjust to in such quick order. We felt as if a warm coat had suddenly been put over our cold bodies.

Miss McAffee, the fourth-grade teacher, introduced us in a short but right-to-the-point manner.

"Children," she explained "we are indeed fortunate to have with us today world travelers from America who have come to talk to you and bring you a gift."

The uniformed students rose automatically and wished us a rousing good morning. Required or not, we enjoyed it.

Rudy moved to the front of the room. "We have brought you art and notes from our United States students," he began, an introduction familiar to me, having heard it in so many schools around the world. He continued, as I took a deep breath knowing he might now be on dangerous territory. "We also were given permission to offer you the art of children in the Irish Republic. They have offered their work freely, and if you would care to receive it, please raise your hand."

Without hesitation, all hands were raised and my regular breathing returned. As we held up each piece of art from what we often heard referred to as "the other side," the students became extremely attentive. The paintings, even though from the Irish Republic, depicted burning trucks, city fires, and boarded-up buildings. Some, of great contrast, showed Ireland's rocky terrain and vast areas of what looked like a green carpet.

Sometimes the American children's art looked too light-hearted by comparison. One painting was a very authentic rendition of Superman with arms extended in flight and his red cape whizzing behind him. These children were especially excited over a painting, that nearly filled the page with our then-famous U.S. football player called "Refrigerator."

"That's America to these kids," we said to each other, half amused.

The students were becoming so excited that Miss McAffee was forced to intervene. "Either we have order presently," she admonished, "or our famous American visitors will go home with tales of misbehavior." This ultimatum was delivered with a twinkle in her eye she could not completely hide. "They are truly my darlin's," she confessed to us privately.

When we admired the Belfast children's clown paintings, the teacher asked if her students would care to have us bring some home. The children all rose, carrying chairs with them, and climbed up in front of their paintings to take them down from the wall. They joyfully offered them to us. As we were packing up our children's art treasures and preparing to leave, a shy little boy named Shane approached me with his prized bag of marbles. "Would you like one for keeps?" he asked. I hesitated until Miss McAffee whispered to us.

"Take one, he means it with all sincerity." Reaching into the bag, I could only hope I hadn't taken his favorite. After hugging several little Colleens whom Miss McAffee had chosen to help us carry our portfolios, we reluctantly walked to our car.

There's not a pilot in the world who would hire me as a co-pilot. My sense of direction is something Rudy has never counted on, but without the aid of our Dublin TV partner, I had to take the map job while Rudy took the wheel. And this had to happen in Wales, which has names no American can read! I was once more in a position to test the strength of a so-far resilient marriage.

Our first contact was with the school art director in Llandrindod, a charming man who resembled Richard Burton. A new school headquarters was being built, and we walked up endless flights of stairs in a 100-year-old home, temporarily housing a Mr. Derek Law, the school principal. We were panting upon arrival at his tiny attic room, but it was well worth the climb. Our Welsh connection made us feel as if Mr. Law's meeting with us was one of the highlights of his life. The welcome was overwhelming, and the tea delicious. Crumpets came in short order. He had charted schools for us in the morning and afternoon.

With a knowledgeable driver taking us to our destination along the beautiful Welsh countryside, life was once more sweet. All I knew about Wales was from the American movie *How Green Was My Valley*. Wales was far from solely drab mining towns. Driving in the countryside made me want to paint every rust and lavender hillside and valley.

After more tea or coffee, Mr. Law asked if we would like to visit his favorite farm school. We jumped at the chance after his insistence on having more tea and crumpets. Passing signs like Caernarvon, Llanelly, Aberdare, Aberystwyth, I was more than grateful that I wasn't reading the map for Rudy.

We were totally unprepared for this farm area's well-equipped art department, dedicated instructor, and creative student's art. I talked to one shy student about her colorful butterfly paintings.

"I paint butterflies," she said, "because insecticides have killed all our real ones." This sad comment made her gift all the more precious. She was overjoyed when we explained we would work hard to get their beautiful art into the most impressive shows in our United States.

The hospitality of these people is something we will never forget. Meeting with their children allowed us to have an understanding of the Welsh in a way we would never have realized had we just been average travelers viewing their lovely country from our rented car.

Once home we kept our word to these children. After much negotiating, we have shown their art in the United Nations in New York, the beautiful Frank Lloyd Wright Civic Center in California's Marin County, and the San Francisco City Hall. My only regret is that I could not personally tell one talented student how far her butterflies have flown.

Ogilvy and Mather, the publisher of our Paintbrush Diplomacy brochure, had arranged a newspaper interview with us through its Edinburgh office. We barely made it down to the lobby in time, where journalists awaited us. Hotel occupants had quite a show seeing Rudy and me on the lobby floor with our children's art spread out all around us while a delightful news photographer snapped pictures. (I always have to remind myself that the way I look is not as important as the children's art. By the end of one of our trips, when I'm looking travel-stained, bedraggled, and weary, it takes detachment to allow news-photos of one's self. Only professionals can afford media grooming.)

Before we left San Mateo, when our daughters and granddaughters realized we would be in Scotland, I consented in a weak moment to buy all of them tartan plaids for Christmas. So each child had to submit to lying on brown wrapping paper, clad only in underwear, while I drew her outline. Once I have these body patterns cut out, folded, and labeled, I'm safe for sizes anywhere in the world.

There's no returning merchandise. Where language is a problem, laying patterns out and using a little hand language, gets the job done. When I laid all five of my patterns out in one small shop, the owner, realizing that she was about to make her quota for the day, simply closed shop. I thus had time to make my purchases in a leisurely fashion.

After visiting the Edinburgh schools on our list, we were once again on the Scottish roads in our new, strange, rented French car. The Scottish brogues were getting more difficult to decipher as we pursued country schools. Our destination was a high school in Perth with delightful, serious-minded art students between 14 and 18. All were preparing art portfolios for their term grades, so we did not want to delay them. We only wished we had more time, but they brought us in to present our American art gift and to explain a little about Paintbrush Diplomacy. They could not know then, nor could we, that their art would be shown with our collection in the United Nations Plaza show at a future time.

We thoroughly enjoyed the Scottish people, but Californians may never be strong enough for their harsh weather. Even with woolens, I turned blue when the air hit like a knife. The people were surprised and pleased to have us because of our art gifts and also because their tourism was down as a result of the Chernobyl explosion, whose fallout might have drifted their way. We had a layover in Glasgow—no schools were booked for us. Our 200 pieces of American art were all delivered. We never trusted airline baggage with it, so Rudy's tired arm could finally rest. Back in our last hotel room, we started wrapping up our mission.

Where to put everything—all the Irish, Welsh, and Scottish art, the gifts for family and friends, and whatever else Rudy and I thought was worth bringing home? We got heavy string and somehow tied things together. We looked forward to Ireland's Shannon airport the next day and then on to home turf and sunny California skies.

"Imagine handling that wind in kilts!" I said to Rudy, but he didn't answer. He was already soundly asleep, with his head against the plane window.

HONOR FROM THE PRIME MINISTER

Olso, Norway—1986

Norway

Over the years we have donated portions of our children's collection to UNICEF. They have made cards with Paintbrush Diplomacy's Chinese and American Indian art. This brought us to the attention of a Norwegian couple, the Goldens. They, too, collected international children's art and had finally found a heaven-sent home for it in Oslo, Norway.

"Lucky people," I told Rudy. "If only we could have such a home for Paintbrush Diplomacy's art!"

His favorite response followed these thoughts of mine. "The last chapter hasn't been written yet, Char."

A huge opening for the culmination of Alla and Rafael Golden's years of work was planned, and many young artists from around the world were invited to attend. Rudy and I were probably the oldest people to receive invitations. We became 10 years younger just thinking about it.

It doesn't take us long to get ready to respond to such offers, and this one was no exception. A few woolens thrown into a suitcase and a quick dip into the "coffee-can savings" did it—the roof still leaked.

Upon arrival in Oslo on September 24, 1986, we were met by hard-working Alla Golden who, before depositing us at our living quarters, drove us to the Children's Museum for a preview. Imagine unlimited grounds covered with greenery forming a backdrop for a three-story, very old white Scandinavian home turned into a children's gallery! As we approached, all I could think of was Santa's elves busily preparing for Christmas. People were working in every possible way to put up international children's art. Each floor was painted a different prime color with white woodwork and wainscoting. Children's puppets hung from the ceilings and their paintings covered the walls. Each stairway brought us to a new level of enchantment. Outside, to the left of the gallery's entrance, was a colorful circus tent in readiness for possible inclement weather. Every detail had been planned, almost entirely with the help of volunteers. Had I not been on jet lag and travel-weary to the bone, I could have enjoyed everything much more, but more might have been too much. I was quite overcome as it was. "Now to rest and find your room," Alla said.

Our housing was on a university campus surrounded by tall trees and scenic walk-ways. The clean, crisp aroma of pine needles filled the air. "A Hollywood celebrity should bottle this. He or she would make a fortune," I told Alla.

Our dorm was filled with guests from Turkey, India, France, England, Ireland, Senegal, and many other countries. Among the guests from Canada was a group of Indians from Alberta. Rumor had it that they were planning a slumber party with the Senegalese students. What a powwow that could be!

We were in awe of the international setting of our living quarters. Early morning started with listening to the Moslem prayer chant of our immediate Turkish neighbors. Walking to the elevator for breakfast, we were greeted by Senegalese girls in beautiful dresses sitting on hall floors, making corn-row braids of each other's hair. Their lovely brown bodies were a complement to their colorful clothing and intricate coiffures. A door left slightly ajar near the elevator allowed a one-inch view of a young American ballerina on her toes, holding on to a bathroom towel bar, stretching her dancer's legs.

Breakfast in our dorm, which Rudy and I referred to as the "international mixer," brought people of all different countries together. Over a bowl of Norwegian gruel, we joined an Irish school principal from a Belfast boys' school and his beautiful Indonesian wife. Like so many of the hospitable, enthusiastic Irish, he soon invited us to visit him, move into his home, and meet his schoolboys. "Oh, to be 30 years younger," I sighed, "with unlimited finances and time for all!"

When I mentioned my feelings to our breakfast companion his blue eyes shone as he responded, "Ah, and surely wouldn't this bring heaven a little closer?" We all knew the answer.

The afternoon brought still another response from the advertising company of Ogilvy and Mather's Norwegian branch office, thanks to Gordon Kallio, then manager of their San Francisco office. They had set up a connection in a nearby school as well as a radio interview for us. Everyone in Norway seemed to speak perfect English, so a translator was not necessary.

At this time "California valley-girl talk" was popular in Southern California, so when I refer to perfect English it's with tongue in cheek. My granddaughters had to translate for me such valley-girl expressions as "grody to the max," meaning gross or unappealing to the maximum.

My language "abilities" in other countries always shame me with my broken Spanish and slangy English. Rudy's respectable English and German language abilities leave me in a constant state of envy.

In thanks for the kindness of the advertising people, we gave their young directors two student art pieces from our wonderful Indio, California, high-school students. Their teacher, Garth Uibel, has helped us expose U.S. high-school students' art in many of our international stops. We just hope his students appreciate him enough; we certainly do. Giving our U.S. art gifts to children of other nationalities always makes the heart pump a little faster on both sides.

The people we talk to the world over always seem anxious to continue cooperating with our simple idea. "Maybe that's why it works," I told Rudy. "It's so simple that people with outstanding gray matter might not have thought of it."

"Now wait a minute," he answered, wondering if he'd been insulted or complimented.

Having kept our people-commitments, we decided to take a scenic train ride to Trondheim. Who could go to Norway and not explore a few fjords? Sometimes in our work with Paintbrush Diplomacy, we get so involved with people (big and little) that we hardly see the country we are in. Missing the beauty of Trondheim would have been like going to India and skipping the Taj Mahal. This train ride whetted our interest in Norwegian scenery so much that we went one step further the next day and took a two-day ferryboat excursion to Bergen.

The ferryboat passengers looked pale compared to us, and their little groups stayed closely together, reminding me of an old movie called *Last Year at Marienbad*, in which all the "right people" returned yearly to their favorite spa and no outsider ever broke in. They looked like wax sculptures by the end of the movie. We tried always to speak softly and never break the spell.

The train ride back to Oslo was much more relaxing for us, and we could better enjoy the country in all its glory. Over the years I've decided that sea voyages weren't my kind of thing, anyway.

Returning to the Goldens' opening celebration, we found the momentum building, and an aura of excitement hung over our dormitory. Much practicing was going on behind the scenes, as the children involved in the lively arts would perform the night of the gallery opening.

When the long-awaited opening day finally arrived, crowds came from everywhere to view the great white home-turned-gallery in the middle of a forest. We will never forget either the road to the gallery lined with kilted young bagpipers or the driveway covered with a real red carpet. As if this were not enough, a huge papier-mâché cow rested in the grass, and decorations graced every doorway. Media people were everywhere.

Finally the procession began. Norway's Prime Minister Gro Harlem Brundtland, a gracious lady, started the parade with other dignitaries following. Behind them came children from around the world in their native costumes. Rudy and I were certainly secondary VIPs but we were still so honored to be part of this whole celebration that even the cold Norwegian wind hurt only slightly.

The Goldens were close to a state of exhaustion but they still worked up to the last second. Like Rudy's and my Paintbrush Diplomacy, this had become a driving force for them. Having migrated from the Soviet Union, Alla's producer husband, Rafael, had been allowed to leave Russia to make documentary films only if his children stayed behind. Unable to visit them, he turned his grief into fostering the creativity of the world's children.

When Prime Minister Brundtland finished her wonderful speech, she said, "And from the United States with their program, Paintbrush Diplomacy, I present Mr. and Mrs. Rudy Pribuss." I was immobile, frozen to the spot where I stood. It was sheer panic and had nothing to do with my frozen feet being glued to the cold ground.

The crowd indicated we should go up to the podium and speak. Fortunately, Rudy pulled me along. I started to thank everyone for having us, but when they announced our representing the United States, my patriotism overcame me, my eyes filled. I felt as though a doorknob was lodged in my throat. Rudy rallied. We smiled, shook hands with and thanked all around us while presenting the Prime Minister with our U.S. art gift. I still can't believe any of it really happened!

After the ceremony, two lovely people came and introduced themselves to us as Ambassador Robert Stuart and his wife from our U.S. embassy in Norway. Shaking hands with us, he said, "We congratulate both of you for the fine thing you are doing in the world and wish more people would do the same." Meeting our countryman who was representing the United States in Norway was just one more joy. He and his wife seemed the perfect ones for the position they held. Once again I was so moved by this unexpected encounter that I had to work hard at looking cool and composed. It wasn't easy at all.

During our last breakfast in the "international mixer," we became involved with some Turkish media people. They were so anxious to have us bring Paintbrush Diplomacy to Turkey's Children's Art Festival in May that their offer looked tempting—as most such offers look to us.

"All we need is a good rest and money," we laughed.

"We can arrange rooms, some plane help and everything," they enthused.

Little did I know that three years later we would go to Turkey to talk in an Ankara high school, thanks to the efforts of a small Turkish travel agency called "Angel Tourism."

"Angels can be helpful," I told Rudy

Leaving Norway, our next and last stop was at a school in Eskilstuna, Sweden. As charming as it was, nothing could compare with the Norwegian enchanted cottage. I still have dreams that a big American Daddy Warbucks has left Rudy and me such a place where all Paintbrush Diplomacy's art might have a permanent home for schoolchildren in the United States to enjoy and learn from. "Oh well," I remind myself in the dream, "the last chapter hasn't been written yet."

MATES AND WALKABOUTS

New Zealand and Australia—1987

Sydney, Australia

We had tried to prepare ourselves for "toughing it out" on the 16-hour flight to Auckland, New Zealand, which started in San Francisco airport at 11:00 p.m. Little did we know we would have a two-hour layover in Hawaii and another in Sydney before arriving at our destination. Twenty-two hours of travel has only one redeeming feature—it feels so good when it stops!

After such an exhausting flight, one might think we went to bed and slept for a couple of days. How could we when we were greeted at 10:00 a.m. the next day by a most charming, gracious Rotarian with a handful of New Zealand schoolchildren's art? We ushered him into our disheveled room littered with our half-opened bags and art portfolio, sat him down on an unmade bed with rumpled nightclothes, and felt an immediate camaraderie. None of us was the least concerned as we had a universal bond going for us, held together by children and art. It canceled out all social norms.

We discussed our aims and Paintbrush Diplomacy's simple format in school classrooms as well as our desire to encourage other travelers to become traveling Paintbrush Diplomats. Our new friend was so responsive that we felt confident.

With a good-sized package of U.S. art and a generous package from our Rotarian friend, we wondered if Rudy's carrying arm could get some assistance. Going to our proven friend, the U.S. consulate, we wound up with their promise to send art by diplomatic pouch and to arrange a newspaper interview. We had discovered that news items stimulate interest in the program, and unlike TV interviews, news clips are often torn out for future notice, allowing people to call us months later.

Thanks to Mary Robbins of Ogilvy and Mather, a San Francisco contact, we were taken to a school where children of many cultures watched what Rudy and I sometimes refer to privately as our "dog and pony" act. We are quite a team with

6' 2" Rudy, 5' 2" Char, our children's art bag, and stories of our worldwide experiences. All we know for sure is that our presentation is never the same— the children's excitement and interest seem to lead us where we go.

The art of the Maori children particularly attracted me with its use of flowers, leaves, and subjects taken from the elements depicting the beauty of nature. We were taken to a beautifully done Maori floorshow presenting their dance, costume, and painted faces (with tongues protruding to scare away the evil one). It was so revealing of their culture that our presence almost seemed an intrusion on their privacy.

We took a small plane from Rotorua to keep a school appointment in Wellington. Until we hit this area, I had thought Chicago was the windy city. The buildings had something of the flavor of our San Francisco Victorian houses, but the wind seemed to swirl around every inch of them. We had a TV interview and a news story, and we spoke to some charming, very enthusiastic children. They told us their morning was much more exciting than the usual three R's, and to please come back often. They acted as if our journey was just a few minutes away.

Our trip to beautiful, rugged South Island was to be for rest and recuperation, we told ourselves. We took a bus ride to Milford Sound's fjords, enjoying the wonderful rugged countryside along the way. Snow-capped mountains, baby lambs, and blossoms were everywhere. "We can say without question that our area has more sheep than people," our bus driver said with a deep belly laugh.

This was their spring season, and we decided that when the cold season came to this harsh area, the people would have to be pretty hearty or there would be only sheep!

A long layover in the Christchurch airport allowed us to review our notes and upcoming contacts in the next stop, which would be Sydney, Australia. Airports have often served us as our own private offices and bedrooms. We can sleep sitting up, standing up, and once we even slept on the cold floor of an Alaskan airport.

"We're either going to get tougher or deader from all this," I once told Rudy, when we sat up all night in a Saudi Arabian airport—Islamic culture does not look approvingly on a man and woman sleeping together publicly.

On our arrival, Sydney, where it was hot and tropical, looked like a little bit of heaven to us, since the colder parts of New Zealand had left us with head colds that promised to slow us down if we didn't nip them in the bud. These were the times when we could be tempted to pull the covers over our heads after a bowl of Australian chicken soup and get off the world for a while; notes in our hotel box, however, dictated otherwise. The ever-loyal Rotary Club had left a phone number and a welcome message. The minister of education would like an appointment, and Sydney's "Today Show" wondered if we could be on their morning program. Could we be at the television studio at 7:00 a.m.? Usually we sleep extremely well on our trips, whether in heat or cold, on "valley mattresses" or lumpy mattresses, or even listening to nibbling mice in China. We awakened on somebody's time (not ours), but when the desk called we were ready.

Every American should have the experience of a TV interview with friendly, quick-moving "mates" of Australia. We laughed a lot and so did they. "Are they laughing with us or at us?" Rudy wondered.

"I don't care. I'm never sure how serious they are, but I love to hear them carry on, and I hope they feel the same about our foolishness."

We parted, telling them our next destination was Papua New Guinea. Their response was, "Don't go there! They'll rob your men and rape your women!"

"We're booked in," we said, "and you can always feel comfortable knowing you warned us if you never again hear of two American Paintbrush Diplomats."

For the first time I saw no frivolity in the look they returned.

We lay wide-awake in a bed of perspiration the night before flying to Papua New Guinea. Having no concrete evidence of a contact there was not the most fortifying feeling. Sitting zombie-like in the airport at that early hour and looking into each other's sleepless eyes was not the world's biggest upper.

"No turning back," I told Rudy. "What could we tell the children in the San Francisco Day School who spent days making masks for us to bring to the children in Papua New Guinea?"

"Who's turning back?" he asked. "Who's turning at all? I think I got a stiff neck lying next to that open window last night."

"THE MUD MEN"

Papua New Guinea—1987

Papua New Guinea

Fascinated by a picture in our travel folder of the Mud Men of Papua New Guinea, I realized that my love of making mud pies as a child was calling me to these people. Their decorated mud-covered bodies and papier-mâché head masks set my creative wheels spinning. Because the first leg of our journey Down Under was to Australia and New Zealand, we told ourselves Papua New Guinea was so close that a stopover was a must.

It was difficult to leave the fun loving Aussies and hospitable New Zealanders for an area some told us was apt to offer dangerous encounters.

"Too late to turn back," I reminded myself as we boarded a small plane for Port Moresby, the capital of Papua New Guinea. Accompanying us were young adventurous-looking backpackers, wearing boots and Aussie felt hats with the left brim turned smartly back. On this last leg of our journey, we just looked weary and wrinkled by comparison—but still felt fresh at heart.

We were close to fearless. Our mosquito-sized plane flew us over dense jungle as bits of clouds drifted through our nonpressurized aircraft. Luggage was piled everywhere, so we each used a duffel bag for a seat. Our pilot turned out to be a New Zealander without a license who was piling up air time. The landing runway was not much more than a gravel pathway cut into the enveloping vegetation. Several serious bumps accompanied by a sputtering engine preceded our landing. As we walked down the plane's tiny exit ramp, we became enveloped in a steam-like atmosphere.

After a monumental delay, we finally arrived at our Port Moresby hotel. It was the only modern-looking structure in sight. Reminders of World War II still remained in the form of tin-roofed shacks, Quonset huts, and Papua New Guineans wandering around in timeworn U.S. army fatigue jackets. I could certainly appreciate what some of our young army engineers lived with while building streets and bridges in this hot, dry area. The natives had a listless look about them, but sweltering heat soon gave us the same look.

"We may be bringing the first connection here since those soldiers left, in the form of their grandchildren's art," I said.

Rudy, a Navy man during the war, looked at the dry and desolate scene and half smiled. "Yeah, at least we had the water and a sea breeze."

In our simmering bedroom, we went through our papers to find what credibility we had for our visit. How to get where we want to go becomes the big question at such times. Melting in our quarters with an overhead fan circulating the steaming air, we were anxious to get on with our mission of delivering a gift of American student art to the children. Out of our disheveled-looking attaché case came our California Congressman Tom Lantos' letter of introduction, explaining the arrival of two Paintbrush Diplomats, and asking our embassy people to give their excellent work every consideration. However, the embassy's answer when we phoned was far from positive.

"I'm sorry, the ambassador is in Washington, D.C., and his assistant is in Australia."

"I wish I were in Alaska," I moaned when I got the word.

"He said the man in charge has only been here two months," Rudy informed me, "and he had no notice of our expected arrival."

A San Francisco school had created masks for the mask-oriented people of this area. Such ingenuity deserved to be enjoyed by its recipients. Unfortunately our U.S. representative was not as enthusiastic as we were about connecting us with a local school. "I have no record of your mission," he said in a voice sounding half amused and half intimidated by a couple of San Francisco pseudodiplomats.

We were later informed of his impending engagement celebration and all that this event involved. Ah, love! After listening to a few half-hearted explanations of his only being a stand-in for the regular representative who would not be back for a week, mild-mannered Rudy said, "Our students have worked long hours on their gifts and we have made many sacrifices to come here. I have copies of our credibility papers," he continued, "and I will bring them to your office. We will be waiting for your call back!"

The phone rang in five minutes—they happened to have found our letter— a car was out in front of our hotel in ten minutes. We were on our way to a school —with tiny American flags flying on either side of the State Department car to announce our arrival. "We're taxpayers," I whispered to myself, clutching our children's art with joy in my heart and my motherly instincts intact.

Never again will I make light of Rudy's paper collecting. Letters with official-looking seals do open doors. The older I get the more I appreciate such backup. Our U.S. government man did not have a sweet face. I tried to bring him a few laughs from the outside world, but his smile reflex was definitely not working.

After driving through a lot of very rural-looking country and back roads, our third U.S. embassy representative got us to our first school in Papua New Guinea. We felt like VIPs as we entered the classroom. Strung from the ceiling rafters were

Peru Age 4

Peru Age 12

Peru Age 15

Poland Age 10

Poland Age 11

Poland Age 13

Poland Age 14

Poland Age 15

Qatar Age 11

Qatar Age 8

Saudi Arabia Age 4

Saudi Arabia Age 8

Saudi Arabia Age 9

Saudi Arabia Age 13

Scotland Age 16

Scotland Age 16

Scotland Age 15

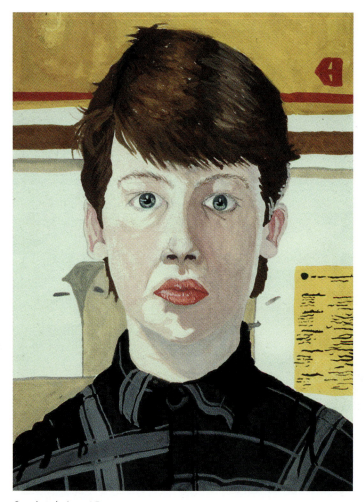

Scotland Age 15

Scotland Age 14

Sri Lanka Age 10

Sri Lanka Age 11

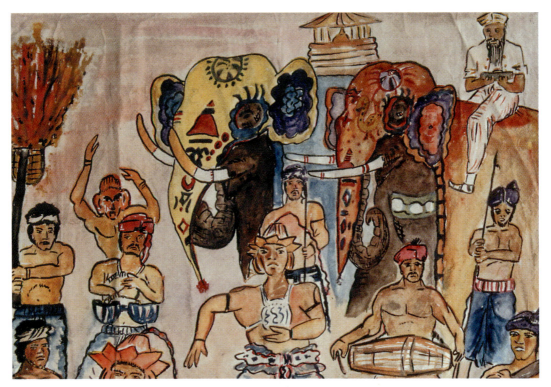

Sri Lanka Age 14

Sri Lanka Age 10

Sri Lanka Age 15

Sri Lanka Age 12

Sri Lanka Age 15

Sweden Age 13

Swed" class="n Age 16

Sweden Age 10

Sweden Age 13

Sweden Age 13

Taiwan Age 13

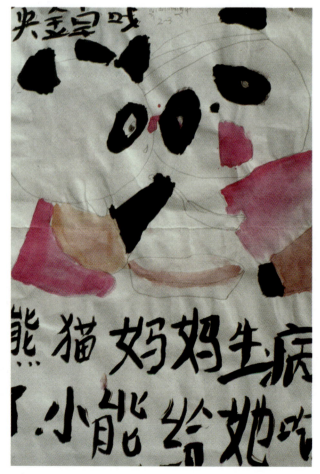

Tibet Age 12

Turkey Age 14

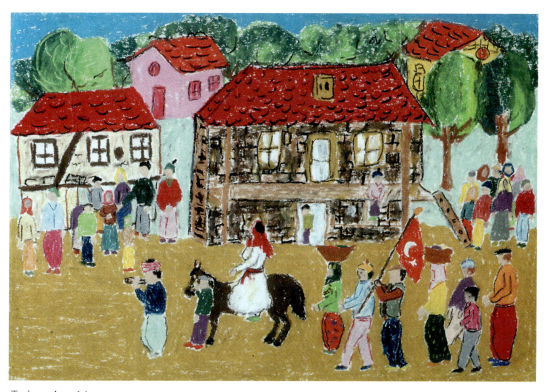

Turkey Age 14

Turkey Age 9

Turkey Age 14

brightly painted paper fish similar to those we had seen at the Great Barrier Reef. The children were seated in a classroom looking quite shy. The girls sat rather primly in white and blue check cotton jumpers, and the boys wore white shirts and dark blue short-shorts. All were barefooted. I wish I could have been! A little good ventilation anywhere would have felt great.

After a brief explanation to the children and teacher about our program, we dug into our U.S. art gift bag, pulling out the masks. The students shrieked with laughter when we gave them the U.S. students' masks. Like everywhere else in the world, faces lit up, and we never saw so many gorgeous white teeth housed in generous smiles. The San Francisco Day School had supplied us with masks laced with various mouths (some smiling, some scowling, some crying) that could be pulled back and fourth giving the impression of smiles, sadness, or fright. Papua New Guinea masks are world famous but the San Francisco children's representation was what we grandparents call "a knockout."

When we told them of our riding elephants (a story we often resort to when there is a need to soften up an audience), they were on our side. Even our U.S. companion started to thaw when he saw the enthusiasm of the children. The children's gift to us was the brightly colored fish we had seen hanging from the ceiling, interspersed with blue paper strips of water that waved as the door opened. A native dance performance by the students followed, and then our representative indicated it was time to leave.

As we walked to the car, we had to check through a rather surprising security system. Suddenly, a hand-rung bell announced recess time. Glancing back into the schoolyard, we saw the children lined up against one side of the building with tin buckets. Each student took one, filled it with water and proceeded to douse the feet of a friend, shrieking with laughter

"Looks pretty tempting," I said, hoping Rudy might kick off his shoes with me, but a look at our official companion threw a wet blanket on this thought immediately.

"God knows what he would have done if he ever saw you doing your girlhood 'trucking' dance for the children in Bhutan!" Rudy whispered.

Our last stop in Papua was a visit to the Mud Men. An overnight in Goroka made me realize why we had an iron security fence around our compound with advice from other travelers to remain indoors at night. We acquired a guide and a ride in a Land Rover referred to by another American adventurer as a "bladder buster." This would be just a side excursion, I told my somewhat doubtful husband. "I saw a picture of the Mud Men in our *National Geographic* magazine and we can't afford to miss this."

"Maybe I can afford it." Rudy smiled, swatting two mosquitoes at once and mopping his brow at the same time.

All's well that ends well, and driving through the Mt. Hagen Range to the Mud Men was an experience in itself. Natives in every small village waved and seemed overjoyed to see us as our Land Rover passed their compounds. A look at little thatched roofs on huts clinging to sheer drop-off hills made even a bladder-buster bus trip worth it. Ah, but the Mud Men was the "big one." "They're here, Char," Rudy said, "just like the *National Geographic* promised you."

Out of the bushes came the Mud Men with huge full head-masks, their bodies completely painted in gray mud, flashing 10-inch-long bamboo fingernails, supposedly to scare off enemy tribes. As they came closer to us, I wondered if we had bitten off more than we could chew. I told Rudy, "I'm not sure this is worth it!"

We instantly recalled our friendly TV interviewers' warning. Memories of stories regarding young Rockefeller and Amelia Earhart never being seen after they hit New Guinea flooded my mind.

Not for long did I hang back, however, and I even had my picture taken with some mud arms embracing me. This great treasure got stuck in the camera, of course, but the experience is stuck in my brain forever.

The Mud Men's bamboo fingernail extensions clicked rhythmically as they led us to their marvelous mud-baked artifacts. All were made of their gray-brown earth. Necklaces of tiny shells held pendants of clay, carefully etched with dancing Mud Men. Their delicacy and careful execution astonished me. Somewhat joking, I whispered to Rudy, "When we get home, throw away my paintbrushes." One of the artists placed a necklace of small shells around my neck. I have worn it many times since, and it always receives rave notices. Making mud pies was never like this.

The chief came out wearing only a World War II jacket (I think), covered with U.S. war medals. Assisted by his subjects, he walked up a dirt mound decorated with beer caps. Later we were told this would be his burial mound. All was done with ceremony, and we showed the occasion our respect. On departure, ex-Navy man Rudy saluted with formality, and the chief returned the salutation with a jaunty U.S. thumbs up! He continued his salute as our bladder-buster Land Rover drove us out of sight. With shining eyes, Rudy looked at me and said, "Now *that* was a chief with class!"

When we headed back to "civilization," I had a feeling of richness that had nothing to do with all the Mud Men's jewelry with which I was adorned.

Early the next morning we were informed that our departure would be slightly delayed. Our driver had apparently met up with a rival gang as we slept in our hammock-type mattresses, and he was now housed in a local jail. No other driver was available, and a replacement would have to be flown in from Port Moresby. "Just think," I said to Rudy. "I could be home now watching the World Series with my San Francisco Giants."

A makeshift bar in the middle of a dirt yard accommodated a few good old boys, Papua New Guinea style. Looking a little closer, I realized that while they drank their local beer, they were glued to a tiny television set. Suddenly a whoop went up from them as Will Clark hit a homer. "What a thrill!" I called to Rudy before returning to my newfound sports buff pals. All was well; word arrived that our chauffeur had been replaced. Even the bladder buster seemed more comfortable the second time around. Anything with four wheels started looking good to us now.

We took a tiny bush-type plane to connect with the airplane in Old Sydney

Port Royal. It stopped at every tiny jungle clearing imaginable and landed on gravel runways no wider than my doormat. Nothing surprised me as once again clouds drifted inside the plane from our window. Baggage was thrown in back of us and acted as a pillow. A 10-year-old Papua boy got off at one stop whose clearing only the pilot could discern. A well-fed joyful grandmother embraced him, and our tiny aircraft once more took off on a runway fit only for a hobby store's model. A native girl became quite airsick across the aisle from me, and I knew then that I had finally received my wings as a seasoned flyer. I felt great!

The long trip from Down Under back to San Francisco International Airport was shorter than going there. We slept a lot of the time and reviewed what seemed several lifetimes. Packed away in the airline locker was our treasure of children's art to share with our U.S. children.

Back in the San Francisco Bay Area, we treated the U.S. kids to a bag of painted fish like none they had ever seen before. They hung them in the classroom windows where they seemed to swim once more in a cool breeze.

Every African American student in the class wanted the address of a Papua New Guinea contact. Some even wanted phone numbers. Thinking of the straw-roofed houses clinging to cliffs that we had recently left, I laughed, "No, phone numbers are *out*."

Recovering from our travel-weary clothes and bodies, Rudy reiterated what I had told myself earlier and what I have heard from him many times. "How rich we are, Char!"

TRAVELING
BACK IN TIME

Yugoslavia, Turkey, Greece—1988

Mykonos, Greece

We left for Yugoslavia September 18, 1988, with the children of St. Catherine's School expecting us to deliver their art and notes to a school in Medjugorje. They had put together art of a spiritual nature as they had heard of a religious experience similar to that in Lourdes presumably taking place there. Rudy and I considered ourselves fairly seasoned regarding the policies of various governments. In this case, however, we soon realized that ignorance and our nonpolitical approach nearly "struck out."

When we arrived, we had the impression the people in this highly spiritual area were quite free to conduct their religious rites. Our concept of Yugoslavia was that—unlike the rest of the communist bloc—they had a relatively free format laid down by Marshal Tito after World War II. How wrong we were! No religious schools were allowed in Medjugorje, and the communist regime had a heavy hand in the monetary intake from tourism, the result of the religious pilgrimages taking place at this time.

A Franciscan monk we approached with our U.S. art quickly hid it under his brown robe, surprising us by saying, "I'm sorry, the schools would throw this away." As Americans, this thought was astonishing.

Disappointed in our rejection, we pondered, "What can we do about the trust St. Catherine's School has placed in us?" Fortunately for us, a wonderful Yugoslavian guide took us to a nearby town where we were met by another young Franciscan monk who had apparently been informed of our program.

We were instructed to hand him our laundry bag full of art. We did so quickly. Thanking the go-between, we immediately got on our bus, and departed. This simple act made us feel like a couple of spies. "Maybe innocence is bliss," Rudy said, slinking down in the seat.

Our mission completed, the next day we left for Ankara, the Turkish capital, where we had a school contact. Taking so many small flights before arriving—waits, naps, bathrooms, or worries over a bout with travel sickness—my numb brain seemed unable to function. Flying and bus riding with motion sickness can make even the most seasoned travelers swear they'd never leave the comforts of home again.

Minutes later, however, all inconvenience was forgotten as we met with the uniformed, excited, English-speaking junior-high students. They completely rejuvenated us as they joyously accepted our gift of cowboy, Indian, and rock star art from instructor Garth Uibel's Indio High School students in the California desert area. They seemed to express the same euphoria as did the students of the Soviet Union when we presented them with blue jeans. We Americans hardly realize how accustomed we are to our daily "perks."

Showing photos of our grandchildren to a few Turkish boys encouraged one to shyly ask for our 12-year-old granddaughter's address and phone number. "Don't laugh too hard," Rudy reminded me. "The world is growing smaller and smaller, quicker than we think, and this kid may be on our front doorstep when we get home."

After completing our school appointment in Ankara—having our picture taken with the school principal and waving goodbye to the students—we decided to make an excursion into central Turkey. *Time* magazine had featured an article about this high plateau region of ancient Persia and its marvelous carpets. Later the area was a Roman province that housed the Christians fleeing the Roman soldiers. Biblical tales relating how St. Paul preached to the people of Cappadocia made me feel obligated to visit so historic a spot.

Arriving in Cappadocia with native people pushing and pulling heavy wooden carts, begging aged and fragile donkeys to assist them, and seeing women chopping heavy firewood was like going back into past centuries. We were mesmerized by Moslem chants at regular intervals throughout the day and night. Men sat on balconies drinking small cups of thick black coffee while their women worked.

"Women's Lib, where are you?" I cried to Rudy.

"After drinking this coffee," Rudy laughed, "I don't see how they can sit. It should turn them all into whirling dervishes!"

The following day, we traveled away from the small town of Nevsehir and came to Cappadocia's main tourist attraction in the form of what Rudy and I thought of as ancient condominiums.

They were certainly geological wonders. In reality, they were carved-out sandstone mountains with elaborate floor plans, used by early Christians when the Romans were pursuing them. They contained intricate water systems and eating areas. It was possible for whole communities to live undetected and quite well for months at a time. Some of these ancient condominiums went underground eight levels. Wall paintings in dark hidden places, illuminated only by candlelight, reaffirmed my belief in man's need for art in order to become fully human.

Their cavelike existence made me feel a certain kinship to them, reminding me of backpacking our U.S. art to schools with dirt floors in the countryside of

Brazil, walking the train tracks accompanied by armed border guards, or spending a sleepless night on a tortured mattress.

Getting from Turkey to Athens airport was what we Americans call "a piece of cake," but getting to our Greek cruise ship was like trying to balance the U.S. budget. A taxi strike blocked the buses. Desperation set in.

After an hour of employing every known form of unethical procedure to get transportation, Rudy finally bribed a civilian into getting us to our new home, a Greek cruise ship. Twelve dollars for 12 miles looked cheap at twice the price. We were booked on the wrong ship, but thanks to our Greek driver, all was set right. "It pays to be unorthodox when the chips are down." Rudy beamed.

Once on board our floating palace, we knew it wasn't for us. I sometimes think that Paintbrush Diplomacy has made us too independent to be comfortable in organized groups with our peers. Bells ringing for meals, food, and entertainment almost gave me a skin rash. "We have probably come close to being the world's oldest hippies," I told Rudy. "These people all seem too normal for us."

Fortunately we were seated at a dinner table with an Australian art teacher, a South African woman who ran a kiwi ranch, and an English decorator with a Woody Allen sense of humor. Trading stories each night proved a bonus that almost made up for the loudspeaker booming instructions at us by way of an overexuberant cruise director whom Rudy referred to as Miss Alka-Seltzer.

Visiting Crete and the palace at Knossos gave me more insight into the ancient Minoan civilization than could any history class. Actually seeing the blue Aegean from the hilltop village of Fira on Santorini or from the beautiful harbor of Mykonos, dotted with boats of every description, proved once more that a single picture is worth a thousand words. The marvels of architecture and engineering of Rhodes, the Acropolis, and Ephesus led Rudy to observe, "As an engineer in the modern world, I must bow to this ancient people's abilities. It's almost too humbling."

"We all can stand some of this humbling—I may never paint again—their art is better than mine. An artist's fragile ego doesn't need this kind of grief."

We encountered one more hassle when the Greek "Love Boat" pulled into the dock at Piraeus, the port of Athens. We had been assured that the strike was over, but we wound up once more with a strike that made the first one look like a baby.

I hustled a man with impressive-looking braid on his shoulder—probably a doorman—who managed to crowd us into a minibus with a group of South Africans going in our direction. He looked like a Greek god to me. We have discovered that desperation often leads to the building of cooing friendships with total strangers.

THE MOSLEM WORLD
LIFTS ITS VEIL

Saudi Arabia and Bahrain—1988

Saudi Arabia

Before the 1991 Gulf War, few Westerners entered Saudi Arabia, the holy place of Mecca, without diplomatic or technological qualifications; in 1988 Paintbrush Diplomacy somehow slipped through! We soon became accustomed to white- and black-draped figures, and confirmed what we already knew: All over the world, children and art create a bond.

We carried religious keepsakes from the children of St. Catherine's School, although we had been warned not to bring them into this Moslem world. Nevertheless, we felt that someone up there was watching over us or we wouldn't even be around. Wrapping rosary beads, Turkish prayer beads, and a Frankfort T-shirt in a bag, we took off in good faith.

Only when we got home did we find out how watched over we were. The Pan Am plane we took from Frankfort to Saudi was the fateful one blown up over Lockerbie, Scotland, shortly thereafter.

By the time we landed in Riyadh, Saudi Arabia, we had experienced so many layovers that we hardly knew what was day, night, real, or movieland. Sitting up in the sumptuous airport in Riyadh with its never-ending marble, fountains, and Arabs wearing what looked to us like long white nightshirts, their heads wrapped in red and white checked scarves with black cords holding them on, made us feel like interlopers in a chapter of the *Arabian Nights*. Our eyes closed from time to time from sheer exhaustion, but lying down seemed so unacceptable in this opulent, strange atmosphere that we would hardly have dared even to pass out.

Finally, after a four-hour wait, we boarded our plane to Jedda, surrounded by white-clad Arabs. We sat with a woman completely covered in black, wearing a veil. She later put her glasses over the veil for a little airplane reading in a beautifully decorated book with exquisite Arabic writing. I had to kick Rudy to get his eyes off this scene.

It was all so unreal to me, I settled for just looking straight ahead, trying to appear mildly uninterested. Suddenly I was jarred into consciousness as the Moslem prayer to Allah came over the loud speaker to assure us a safe landing.

"I'll take whatever good wishes they have," I told Rudy when the slightly jerky landing ended smoothly.

Waiting at the security gate, still standing out like two sore thumbs, I said, "The U.S. Information Agency people said a U.S. consulate person or 'one of our own' would meet us." Still surrounded by a white tent of people, we didn't see anyone who fit this description. Nowhere did I hear the sound of my native language. I panicked. Suddenly a Western-dressed Arab appeared, and in desperation, I said, "I hope you're looking for us!"

"My name is Awaken, U.S. Information Agency Expediter," he smiled. "I am your expediter and I will take care of everything for you." He handed me his card that confirmed all. After we got through customs (which proved to be a fast procedure), we realized that somewhere along the line we were considered worth looking out for.

A driver holding a "Pribuss" sign took us to our next contact, U.S. Consul General Jay Frerres. At this point Rudy and I had been sleepless for roughly 24 hours, and Jay and his wife, Maria, had apparently been doing some pacing on our behalf because of the long delay in our arrival. Such lovely people, these! Jay, still in his bathrobe, greeted us with breakfast, a room in their U.S. consulate home, and an offer of an all-day excursion on the Red Sea, thanks to the loan of Mobil Oil's luxurious launch. They explained they were well aware of the sleepless ordeal we had been through and said they certainly would understand if we could not accept their invitation.

After they told us that some of their friends were looking forward to meeting us, we felt that, dead or alive, we would accept. A shower and change of clothing was all we needed, and we soon found ourselves jumping off the launch with their friends, swimming in the Red Sea, and being waited on as if we were royalty. I loved it all!

We were surprised when the Frerreses got to know us a little better and admitted, "What you people are doing with Paintbrush Diplomacy is impressive to us all, but the way you rallied for the Red Sea outing impressed us the most."

Grand as it all was, I would have traded any of the grandeur for that first night's wonderful, uninterrupted nine hours of sleep. "This is worth all the oil in Saudi," was the last thing I remember Rudy saying as I drifted into my own restful Arabian night.

The next day we were given an itinerary by the U.S. consul that would have choked a couple of 20-year-olds. So much work had gone into the planning for our stay in Saudi and the outlying Arab countries, we would not have considered feeling too old to accept. Apparently, no one was sure just how many schools would be amenable to our Paintbrush Diplomacy program, so they booked more schools than they thought would respond. As it turned out, all responded—plus many more classes beyond those originally scheduled. We had also been told in some quarters that King Fahd had said we were to have full support in our efforts. Exciting, even if only a rumor.

The Arab children were the most talented, the most generous, and the most amazed at our presence of any children we had seen in our 16 years of talks. Saudi is a very private society and has almost no tourism, so their children were delightfully receptive and enthusiastic.

They greeted us with bouquets of flowers and pungent offerings of incense. Their home economics classes presented us with cakes, knitted baby garments, and any artwork we admired. What our arms could not carry, they offered to send. Every child wanted to know that something of theirs would arrive in America.

They loved our U.S. art gifts, but all had been carefully screened. No paintings of girls in low-necked dresses or minidresses were acceptable. In order not to offend the Saudis, I had quickly pulled out my watercolors the night before and sketched some ruffles over bare arms and legs. (Once more, my little travel paints bridged cultural differences.) The children were delighted and no one noticed the additions. Basically, our children's art and theirs was much the same in its honesty and innocence.

Only Rudy could speak in the boys' classes, and only I in the girls'. To be on the safe side, I wore my Minnie Mouse watch that proved to be quite a show-stopper.

We also visited a few schools in the independent state of Bahrain, an island country connected to Saudi Arabia by the King Fahd Causeway. This 15-mile-long causeway had been completed only two years before out visit.

As a result of our visit to Saudi Arabia and Bahrain, the art of their children appeared in many of our local schools, San Francisco International Airport, and the main plaza of the United Nations building, making our strenuous daily schedule worth it. Any physical discomfort is a small price for the many rewards our young people and we have received.

As we left our American and Arab friends, our driver's last message was, "Please come back, and would you mind if I pray to Allah for your safe journey home?" We accepted gratefully.

"EAST GERMANY"
NO MORE

Germany—1988

Rudy and Char in a Dresden classroom

The good German food we ate while living in the boardinghouse was a welcome relief from the food in some Eastern European countries we had visited. No mystery gravy covering mysterious food. The real nourishment, however, was at the table across from us, where a teenager and an old man conversed as if they had never before fully communicated. They hadn't.

My husband, Rudy, was born in what was recently communist-run East Germany. A short time before we arrived in 1988, it had gained its freedom. The young danced on its once-threatening Wall as the older and wiser looked on skeptically. They had lived longer and hurt more. We Americans were euphoric to see all the people who were grasping freedom, wanting to emulate our Western democratic way of life. Most of us had no idea what a luxury this was. We had never lived under anything else but freedom.

Our first morning at a Dresden boardinghouse, we were seated in a small dining room and were served *ein Ei* (one egg), hot rolls (unlike most European countries), and real rib-supporting *Kaffee*. My folksy husband soon started a conversation with the elderly man at the next table. Rudy had retained his German language, thanks to his parents who had always spoken German to him since bringing him to the United States at age four. His Saxon accent, indigenous to the people of Dresden, brought smiles and amazement to these people who until recently were so isolated.

"What is an American doing here speaking like this?" some of them asked.

As the conversation continued, we learned that until now the old man could only occasionally cross from one side of the Berlin Wall to the other. The cement barrier had been fortified with guards and police dogs. He could visit for only a day, leaving his younger wife and grandchildren behind while visiting a grandson who lived in West Germany. At 65, East Germans could leave permanently only if they were considered no longer useful to the communist regime. Now for the first time this teenage boy could come to his grandfather's world for a vacation and truly get to know him. They were traveling all the spots the grandfather could only tell about prior to this.

"So," Rudy smiled, "you have a whole country again and all of the German people can join hands, no longer separated from their friends and loved ones."

The man gave a sort of sad little smile. All Rudy said was true, he explained but so much more was also true. While Rudy translated to me, our friend spoke softly, as if he were still not sure Big Brother was really gone. These people had been so long separated from Western thinking, individual enterprise, and what we Americans call opportunity, that they hardly knew how to begin. An election was on while we were in Dresden, and some German communists were running for office along with the new German aspirants. Tension filled the air, and we were surprised to see Russian military still walking the streets. Their economy was in very sad condition. The people never fully realized this until the Wall came down and they saw what life was about on the other side.

Enterprising young people were leaving for the West. Those remaining were desperately in need of Western guidelines in order to catch up and join the modern world. As Rudy listened and relayed the conversation of the old man, I realized—in a way I never had before—that we Americans are too often unaware of what Old World cultures are about and certainly what these Eastern European people had to deal with. Our news media wrote sensational stories about what freedom meant, but not enough of the downside of these people's plight. The stories we got in Prague, Poland, Estonia, and now Germany, were not too different from one another.

We finally said *auf Wiedersehen* to the grandfather and his teenage grandson. As we left, they continued their animated conversation with each other. The boy practiced a little of his English on me, and I a little of my scanty German on his grandfather. Our no-nonsense Hausfrau and waitress quickly cleared our place, pocketed our tip, and had everything set up for the next morning before we closed the boardinghouse door behind us. "Such efficiency will find a way," Rudy said, as we caught a bus for Ebigow, the little town where Rudy was born.

Unlike our previous visit to Dresden, when we had to replace a car license plate from one German area to the next and undergo a complete police inspection of car and person, we now crossed without incident. We smiled, took a deep breath, and wished these people well.

AUDREY AND I

San Francisco—1992

Audrey Hepburn is honored with African child's painting, Char and Rudy present

In 1992 the UNICEF International Children's Program invited my husband and me to a luncheon at the Fairmont Hotel in San Francisco to honor Audrey Hepburn.

"You will be seated at the head table," we were told, "as co-founders of the international children's exchange program, Paintbrush Diplomacy." Having donated our art for UNICEF's calendar that year, the invitation sounded reasonable to us, but to touch the hand of the woman who was embraced by Gregory Peck—or was it Gary Cooper?—was almost more than my average American hand could accept without trembling.

Somehow I realized before meeting this elegant celebrity that it would be pointless to try to look as lovely as possible. A new outfit would still make her prettier, younger, and more talented than I. The best thing to do would be to wear my good little wool suit, my "real" anniversary pearls, and black Italian Ferragamo shoes. This last touch could make me feel slightly European.

"Oh, God," I told my husband, "if only my mother had given me ballet lessons, I could at least move like Audrey. I should have bought a designer Galiano dress even if we had to mortgage the house."

Our Paintbrush Diplomacy director primed me with a present for Miss Hepburn—a painting recently sent to us by a student from Africa's Maasai tribe.

"Why me?" I asked, as my stomach started to churn with anxiety. How stupid I was to have been caught up in the idea that human beings are all the same except for those with celebrity status. Once introduced, Miss Hepburn put out her hand, grasped my painter's freckled one, and I suddenly realized we were one.

"Tell me how your program started?" she asked. When I told her I was an artist, she lit up. Her gorgeous eyes shone, as I remembered they did when she was embraced by Gary Cooper—or was it Gregory Peck?

"My youngest son is in design school in Rome," she said. From then on we had a bonding. What she wore, her styled chignon exposing her swanlike neck, her stately poised simplicity, drifted from my consciousness. She was totally honest, unaffected, a wonderfully caring person. Her dedication to UNICEF and children like the hungry in Ethiopia was obviously paramount in her life. Her own "Madonna & Child" art graced UNICEF cards that year, as did Paintbrush Diplomacy's

I will long remember our 10 precious minutes.

"This is a great lady!" my husband and I said in unison. There are many great, giving people who are not considered celebrities, and I wonder if we put too much emphasis on what that title really means. Was I in awe of Miss Hepburn? Yes, and I would love to have asked her just how blue Gary Cooper's eyes really were, but I was also in awe of her sisterhood with the rest of us ordinary women.

How unimportant my not-too-comfortable Italian shoes were when her movie-star hand reached out and shook my ordinary one.

I do know our hands knew they belonged together.

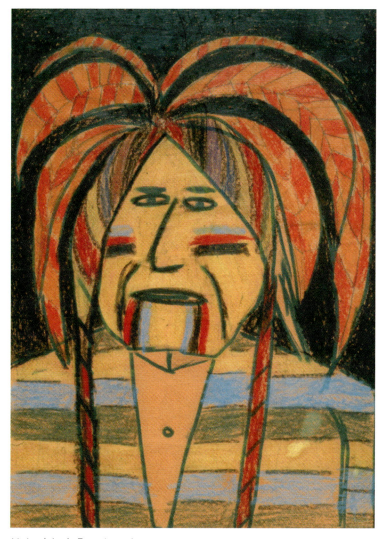

United Arab Emerites Age 11

United Arab Emerites Age 12

United States of America Age 12

United States of America Age 14

United States of America Age 12

United States of America Age 9

United States of America Age 15

United States of America Age 10

United States of America Age 15

United States of America Age 9

United States of America Age 11

United States of America Age 10

United States of America Age 9

United States of America Age 9

United States of America Age 7

United States of America Age 17

United States of America Age 5

United States of America Age 10

United States of America Age 15

United States of America Age 15

Union of Soviet Socialist (USSR) Republics Age 7

Union of Soviet Socialist Republics Age 15

Union of Soviet Socialist Republic Age 13

Union of Soviet Socialist Republics Age 8

Union of Soviet Socialist Republic Age 12

Union of Soviet Socialist Republic Age 12

Union of Soviet Socialist Republic Age 13

Union of Soviet Socialist Republic Age 11

Union of Soviet Socialist Republic Age 14

Union of Soviet Socialist Republic Age 14

Union of Soviet Socialist Republic Age 12

Union of Soviet Socialist Republics Age 13

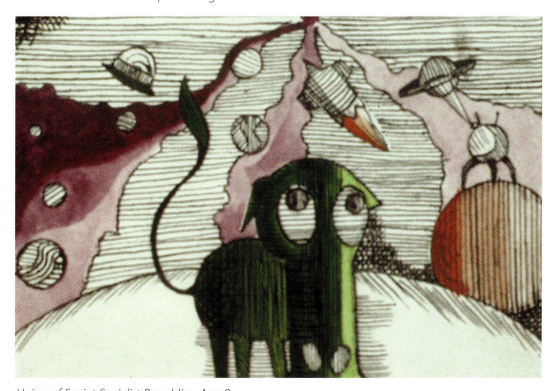

Union of Soviet Socialist Republics Age 9

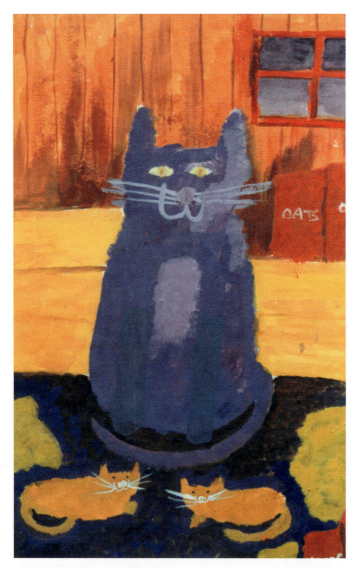

Wales Age 11

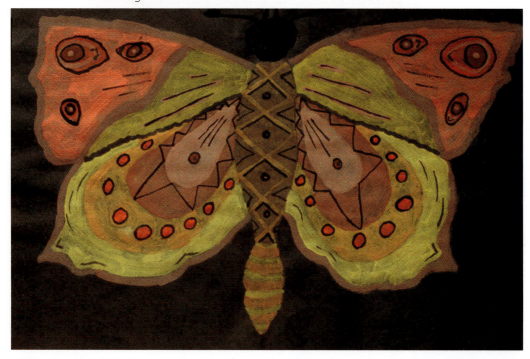

Wales Age 12

Wales Age 15

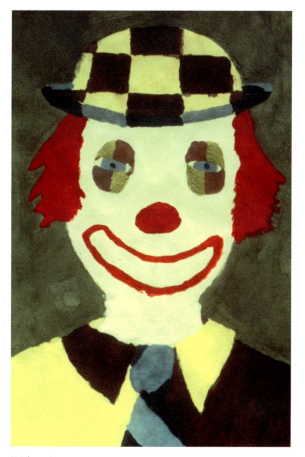

Wales Age 12

Yugoslavia Age 12

Yugoslavia Age 11

NOT ALONE

Rome—1993

Vatican Swiss Guard

After six years of being a Parkinson's disease caregiver for my husband, I was starting to need a "jump start" for my own battery. The thought of a pilgrimage to the shrine of the holy man, Padre Pio, in San Giovanni Rotondo, Italy, tempted me greatly. "Such an emotional vitamin pill this would be," I told myself, until my more practical side took over.

Although Rudy and I had traveled a great deal, his health problems made me reluctant to take the responsibility for another major trip. He now had difficulty getting around, dressing was slow, eating could be a challenge, and his thinking was no longer as decisive as it once was. Despite these roadblocks, San Giovanni Rotondo still lingered in my thoughts one night as I whipped up a spaghetti dinner.

On my early morning walk the next day, I saw my friend Elizabeth Beaulaurier. In the course of our quick conversation, I remembered her meeting with a monk on a trip to Italy a few years back.

"Didn't you go to Rome and visit the holy man, Brother Gino?"

"Oh yes," she glowed, "it was marvelous."

"I would love to do this," I told her, "but time takes its toll, and the bell is starting to toll for me."

Before we parted, she offered some flattering denials of my tolling bell, but my reflection in the store window told me otherwise. Not long after, I again ran into Elizabeth coming out of the market. She was lit up like a Roman candle.

"If I can convince my loving husband, Gerry, to go to Italy, we would come as your support system," she smiled. This did not seem too unusual to me, as I knew her husband's pilot status made gratis flying very enticing to them—they took off periodically. We did a little half-serious speculating, but before I realized what I was doing, the dream was becoming a reality. Not only was a pilgrimage beckoning, but presenting the Vatican with Rudy's and my children's art exchange program,

Paintbrush Diplomacy, looked like a possibility.

"Why not?" our friends encouraged, "the next generation is our best hope."

A phone call from Gerry saying he was ready for some real Italian pasta made me feel closer than ever to our dream. Their slot for take-off was three weeks from our meeting. I had no time to waste.

Suddenly things moved us without our having to do the moving. Father Miles Riley, head of communications for the San Francisco archdiocese, heard of our Paintbrush Diplomacy program and gave me contacts in Rome to the Office of Communications, Città del Vaticano, and to the Pontifical Council for Social Communication.

"That's what your program is about," he said, "getting our young to communicate with their peers around the world."

All I had to do in two weeks was complete packets for each contact, condensing a 20-year program into a few pages. Sometimes the pressure of a fast-approaching deadline works wonders. Never have I put so many thoughts into a medium-sized manila folder.

I was next referred to a Monsignor Steven Otellini who had recently spent time in Rome. He suggested faxing a further condensed page on Paintbrush Diplomacy to the Office of Communications. Receiving my further condensation, he kindly sent it on to Rome. To our surprise, we received a fax back the next day saying we should set up a meeting with them upon arrival in Rome. Now Rudy and I were off and running, at least walking briskly. He had a twinkle in his eye I hadn't seen for a while, and I intended to keep it there.

"No medication can perk you up like this," I laughed. "Rome, here we come!"

We felt quite protected with our support system in the form of our friends the Beaulauriers as the four of us left San Francisco International Airport. We were thrilled to be together and excited at the prospect of our upcoming adventure. All went well until Dulles Airport in Washington, D.C. Rudy and I had to take off alone for the second leg of our journey to Rome, but we had our friends' assurance they would surely get on standby the next day and would meet us at the hotel in Rome. Our next contact with them was a phone call from D.C. saying they had tried getting to us via Brussels, but it was "no go."

"All flights are booked, Char," Gerry said in a sad voice, "we have to return to California."

With tears in my eyes I assured him we would be fine. Our other great blow came when the hotel we thought we were registered in had no knowledge of us but agreed to put us up for a day and a night. The Columbus Hotel became our home for the entire nine days although the matter was never discussed again by anyone, but the first day had looked pretty bleak.

We were two blocks from St. Peter's Basilica and as I sat on my bed after Gerry's phone call, I laid my head back, reached my arms heavenward, and exclaimed, "St. Peter! We need all the help we can get. Please give us a hand."

This trip was a heavy challenge. We had cancellation insurance I considered using. I was beginning to feel like a tightrope walker without a net, but when I thought of the children who had entrusted their art and messages to us, and listened to the robust strains of an Italian waiter under our window bursting his heart in an operatic aria, I looked at Rudy and asked, "What do you say we go it alone?"

"I'm ready," he smiled.

We linked arms and headed for our first Italian pasta and a bottle of red wine. Somehow Rudy seemed to be walking more quickly, and I forgot that his shoulders were not as straight as they used to be. Whose are?

Bright and early the next morning, we were presented with yet another challenge. The archbishop we had our precious contact with was out of town for two days. Hoping to get an audience with the Pope in order to deliver a child's painting and a letter from Poland, along with a poignant war message from a Croatian child, we pointed our feet toward St. Peter's Square. Wednesday was the only day for a Papal audience. Despite being on "California time" the day after arriving, we managed to keep going on three hours of sleep.

The young Swiss Guards at the Vatican, dressed in their colorful gold, red, and blue uniforms, started feeling like our close friends as we kept returning to them for directions. Little by little we started making progress as I waved our fax message from the Office of Communication. Somehow we wound up with two passes for the Papal audience at St. Peter's Basilica.

"We are probably two of a thousand people receiving these," we told each other. As we walked into the huge impressive building, an usher started bringing us closer and closer to the front rows. Crowds formed on all sides. The usher continued bringing us closer and closer to the main altar. When we were finally seated in the second row, I whispered to Rudy, "Let's pretend we deserve this."

I had our gift scroll ready for the Pope but was amused to think we could ever deliver it in this impressive-looking scene. As the Pope came our way, I was almost in a state of shock when I watched Rudy calmly reach out and hand him our gift. His Holiness nodded, smiled, and gave us his blessing. With 10,000 people watching, tears streamed down my cheeks while Rudy and I hugged, and three teenaged German girls, wanting to share our joy, joined our embrace.

The next day we left the remainder of our children's art and letters at the North American Office of Communication and started planning the final challenge, and it certainly proved to be one. Travel agents gave us two totally different approaches to San Giovanni Rotondo, and one well-meaning man said with compassion and a heavy accent, "You don't want go there, it's too hard. Stay in beautiful Rome."

What he didn't realize was that with all we had been through, we were now ready to take on the world. The prospect of bus transfers, train transfers, and no assurance of getting a hotel after a long difficult day's travel made the hotel desk clerk's costly suggestion of hiring a driver look better and better.

"Even if all our remaining 'tip and mad money' goes for the driver, it's better than dropping dead from exhaustion in a strange place," Rudy said half seriously.

I gave him no argument and arranged for a car.

Our driver, Luigi, proved a perfect link to San Giovanni Rotondo. We viewed blankets of red poppies covering the fields, relaxed to the restful hum of the car sporting a little bouquet of flowers in a vase suctioned to one window while the Virgin Mary dangled from the rear view mirror. Sharing our bottled water, we were drunk on a feeling of detachment from the real world.

Arriving at such a poor, unpretentious town as San Giovanni Rotondo, with hoards of visitors from all over the world, was mind-boggling. An aura of peace ran through it. Even the vendors of rosary beads and medals did not diminish our enthusiasm. We walked through the little town, lunched, and spent time in the tiny chapel.

"How could all of this happen?" Rudy said.

"How could we be here?" I pondered.

The many cures said to have taken place here are attributed to Padre Pio, the patron of San Giovanni Rotondo. What the future holds for Rudy's Parkinson's disease we do not know, but we will never forget the privilege of a pilgrimage, a shot of courage, and an experience of a lifetime.

The last day of our nine-day trip we laughed while sitting on the Spanish Steps with the hangers-on from the hippie era.

"The oldest hippies in the world made it again," we said in unison.

We could have stayed home and been prudent, I thought, as I guided Rudy's footing for the last time. Walking the straight and narrow path could not lace the rest of our life with the dreams we have dared to dream.

"Too bad you can't buy such an emotional upper over the counter," I said as Rudy took his allotted Sinemet and Eldepryl medications.

Elizabeth and Gerry's luggage was sent to Rome. They hoped it had a nice vacation.

PASSING ON THE PAINTBRUSH

San Francisco—1997

Sheri Sobrato and Char

Looking back at our life over the past 25 years, Rudy and I smiled as we remembered our first show of Paintbrush Diplomacy's art in a little cultural center in West Virginia.

In 1980 The Smithsonian Institution had taken our Chinese collection throughout the United States for three years. We stopped at some of the exhibits, amazed to see how many people reached out for our efforts, sometimes in the most unpretentious little towns.

When we told people of our experiences in China and how we acquired the art being exhibited, all doors opened. We were brought into their homes and farms with opportunities to see what people were really like in different parts of our country.

For 11 weeks in 1990 during another nationwide exhibit, we drove across the United States, making stops at our exhibits, explaining to people from Seattle to New York our desire to bring the world's young closer together through the universal language of art. For the first time in our married life, Rudy and I took a leisurely look at our own country without our children wanting to get going, stop at a rest room, eat, drink, swim, or fight to sit next to a window. Now they are all grown and on their own, taking their own exotic trips.

When we are together, they often reminisce, laugh, and talk about our family cross-country trips, referring to them as *The Grapes of Wrath* trips—our unmatched luggage roped to the top of the old station wagon and a borrowed air conditioner shooting water through the window on the back seat.

In contrast, Rudy and I considered our U.S. trip alone a luxury we will never forget. We finally understood our vast diversified country in a way we previously had taken for granted.

When telling about our experience, Rudy often said it was the true test of a marriage. "Eleven weeks taking turns driving across the United States, walled into a tiny car, could make or break a marriage," he told more people than I care to think about.

Most Americans, however, seem more anxious to learn our reactions to other countries we have visited than to hear about their own. They always ask, "In your many years of travel, which country did you like the most?" Our answer has always been the same: "In different ways, all of them."

Often the second question is, "Were your ventures always as much fun as they sound?" To that my answer is an honest "No! Some involved hardships, but these were always outweighed by the ultimate joys."

Going back to 1978 when we entered China with a few pieces of U.S. children's art and no representation between that country and ours, we never dreamed where Paintbrush Diplomacy would take us. It didn't even have a name.

Freezing cold and bundled up like panda bears, we had handed out our little homemade print-out sheets, telling our aims to Mao-clad officials in an unheated train compartment. This all seems like a lifetime ago, and in some ways, it was.

Since then, Paintbrush Diplomacy has built another world for us and, we trust, for others who have participated in our program. We have talked to classrooms of young people in over 60 countries of the world and watched their enthusiasm as they reached out for our U.S. student art gifts. We hope that through our efforts they have gained a little more understanding of our country than they acquired through our movies and sit-coms.

Did lasting connections come about through our efforts? Have we had anything to do with the growth of freedom in areas where our early visits evidenced no such hope?

We may never know.

When the Soviets confronted us in 1983 at the time the Korean plane was downed, we had just entered Latvia, a Republic of the Soviet Union. Both our harmless program and our being U.S. citizens looked highly suspect to those in control at this time. We were merely hoping to make a school connection and, because of a five-day news blackout, had no knowledge of the plane incident. Thus we were totally amazed when the helpful-looking people who met with us turned out to be the KGB. They brought us to an imposing-looking old home where we were seated around a large conference table and were interrogated for an hour by high-ranking officials, sliding doors closed behind us.

It was not until Rudy courageously asked whether the actions of any nation, ours or theirs, were always right that the attitude of the KGB men changed, giving me the nerve to say, "Give us a break" Suddenly we were being served tea and cookies and were presented with 25 pieces of Latvian children's art. We were allowed to leave and return to our hotel. A phone call came later from the head interrogator, inviting us to visit his son's school. He would pick us up in an hour.

The camaraderie between the woman principal and me, when she learned that we had both been art teachers, was the best medicine I've ever had! Since then their children's art has been shown from San Francisco International Airport to the

United Nations Plaza, and a link between their children and ours continues through the mail.

Visiting the Mud Men of Papua New Guinea in 1987, made me wonder if we had "bitten off more than we could chew" as they came out of the bushes clicking their bamboo-extended fingernails, their bodies covered with mud. It took a little doing to smile when they embraced me on our departure, but their schoolchildren now trade art with ours. Rudy put it all in perspective when later he said to me, "What's a little mud amongst friends, Char" I prize my mud necklace above diamonds and only wish I had brought home dozens for my more open-minded friends.

Our last major trip was to Saudi Arabia, Bahrain, and Dhahran in 1988, and it was one of the most interesting of all. Being the sole Westerners in Saudi's sumptuous airport, with nobody to meet us and take us in hand, was a frightening experience. When our wonderful U.S. Information Agency people finally arrived, they made me feel like a strong, comfortable woman. The Arab children's artwork continues to circulate in our U.S. schools. Each new packet looks more beautiful than the preceding one.

Looking back to 1986 when our local art community of San Mateo offered to change our dream into a nonprofit corporation, we had no idea what the transformation of an idea into a full-fledged organization would do to our lives.

Maybe it was better that we were ignorant in such matters. Otherwise, we might never have agreed.

All we knew was that our dream had become too big for two people to handle.

Our home was turned into something close to a shopping mall. Phones rang constantly, children's art was stored in our bathtub, my art studio became an office, our tiny cul-de-sac street had a steady stream of cars. Fortunately our neighbors proved to be true friends, still speaking to us by the time we finally moved to a regular office two years later.

I was told to go write a book to help the program, so I turned to a college writing class to comply with the request. I soon learned to appreciate all writers who completed any book, and I was in awe of anyone who got a nod from a publisher.

The board members, executive director, and volunteers of our nonprofit corporation can vouch for the fact that it was all done on "a wing and a prayer." Suzanne Orcutt, our first director, learned with us as we went along. She claimed she was the midwife for Rudy's and my international baby. She didn't coddle it; she programmed it.

Becoming a fund-raiser in my old age is a far cry from being the artist I was before this all hit. The name Paintbrush Diplomacy came from an area of my subconscious I knew nothing about.

Interviewed on TV with no script, we were asked what we called our program. With markers on the floor, TV cameras showing our unglamorous faces, and stage fright taking over, I said, "Oh, we call it Paintbrush Diplomacy,' and so our baby was christened. A name helped put a frame on our dream. It was copyrighted and it stuck.

We became legal in all ways. The program has continued to grow; with growth has come more responsibility, and more people, money, and workers are needed. We sometimes feel we walk a tightrope, but we do manage to keep walking—as do our loyal supporters.

What about the future of these two dreamers who passed their dream to so many travelers and children? We were blessed with a young woman from the San Francisco Peninsula who took up the gauntlet as new head of the board of directors, and we pass the larger part of the torch to Sheri Sobrato with a feeling of great optimism.

She has much the same look in her eye as Rudy and I had when we started Paintbrush Diplomacy. Have we lost that look? People don't seem to think so; we just have a few more wrinkles around our eyes that have had the privilege of seeing so much of this amazing world. We are thrilled as we watch others now build Paintbrush Diplomacy into a substantial program connecting our schools with those of other countries. Will we (or you) ever again leave home without any U.S. children's art at the bottom of our suitcases? I can't imagine such a thing. Our clothes would die of loneliness.

Perhaps California's Carmel Valley, San Francisco's inns, or Sonoma's wine country may be enough for us now, but like the race horse who hears the opening shot and has to run, Rudy and I will still walk with you (if not run) to a challenge. Now, instead of just red, we have all the prime colors running through our veins, but we wouldn't trade for anything less colorful. We often have said to each other, "It's all been too good for these California dreamers," but we also say a humble thank-you to the world and its marvelous young people. "If you call on us, somehow we'll get to you."

THE INTERNATIONAL CHILDREN'S ART MUSEUM

The International Children's Art Museum, based in the San Francisco Bay Area, is an outstanding collection of paintings created by children from over 100 countries. It is the only collection of its kind in the United States. ICAM's mission is to foster understanding of world cultures and promote children's causes through the exchange and display of children's art. Through its exhibitions and products, the museum raises funds for, and awareness of, children's causes nationwide and internationally.

The permanent collection comprises 3,000 works gathered through Paintbrush Diplomacy, the museum's international program for exchanging the art and writings of schoolchildren around the globe. The program fosters artistic expression and promotes cultural understanding through the language of children's art. By pairing American and international classrooms, Paintbrush Diplomacy exchanges more that 8,000 pieces of art annually. Participating children enjoy and learn from the exchange as well as gain satisfaction in knowing that their artwork may be used to improve the living conditions and health of children worldwide.

Appendix A
ACKNOWLEDGMENTS

UNITED NATIONS CHAPTER 1
Honorable Herbert S. Okun, Permanent Representative of the U.S. to the U.N.
    in New York City
Joseph V. Reed, U.N. Undersecretary General for Political and
    General Assembly Affairs
Mrs. Anne Murphy, Wife of Richard W. Murphy, Assistant Secretary of State
    for Near Eastern and South Asian affairs.
Rotary Club
Chevron Oil Company, San Francisco

ARMENIA CHAPTER 3
Director, Children's Art Museum, Yerevan

CHINA CHAPTER 4
Mr. Woo, Tour Conductor, China
Mr. Yee, Tour Conductor, China
Barbara Shannon, Canadian Guide for China

MEXICO CHAPTER 5
Sally and Frank Bolek, Guadalajara
Señor José, Principal, Guadalajara

JAMAICA CHAPTER 6
Ann and Arnold Anderson, Castro Valley, California
Virus, Jamaica
Rob, High-School Teacher, Jamaica
William's Wife and Mother, Jamaica

ALASKA CHAPTER 7
Judy Franklet, Head Start, Juneau
Tlingit Indian School, Juneau
Robbie Benko, Assistant Museum Director, Juneau

HAWAII CHAPTER 8
Millie Wellington, Grade School Teacher, Kauai
Miss Haole, Grade School Teacher, Kauai

INDIA AND NEIGHBORS CHAPTER 9
Leonard Breger, San Francisco
Ishrat and Narsima Aziz, Indian Consul and Wife, San Francisco

Chandra Lother, Indian Reporter, New Delhi
Shankar Children's Art Center, New Delhi
Father Kristy Daniles, San Mateo, California
Mr. Khan, Kashmir Guide
Indian Rotary Club
Maria Scheeley, Bhutan Guide
Father Roberts, Nepal

SCANDINAVIA CHAPTER 10
Vera Maki, San Mateo, California
Timothy Persons, Helsinki
George Kristovich, San Mateo, California
Åsa and Jan Brandt, Torshälla, Sweden
Torshälla Student Art Center, Torshälla, Sweden
Anders Linders, Professor, Swedish Institute, Stockholm
Swedish Cultural Center
Raoul Wallenberg School, San Francisco
Diane Parkhill, Teacher, Raoul Wallenberg School, San Francisco
Margaret, Copenhagen
Edvard Munch Gallery, Oslo

ESTONIA AND LATVIA CHAPTER 11
Tom and Annette Lantos, San Mateo, California Congressman and Wife
Russian Friendship Society, Tallinn
Erica Packman, San Mateo, California
Russian Friendship Society, Riga, Latvia

ESTONIA CHAPTER 12
Toomie, Tallinn
Children's Art Museum, Tallinn

GERMANY AND POLAND CHAPTER 13
Congressman Tom Lantos, San Mateo, California
Mr. and Mrs. Paul Arnold, Dresden
Zwinger Children's Art Center, Dresden
Bronislawa and her husband, TV News, Warsaw
Bronia, Krakow
City of Hope Hospital, Krakow

SOUTH AMERICA CHAPTER 16
Congressman Tom Lantos, San Mateo, California
Lucy Alvarez, Peruvian Cultural Center, Lima
Father John, Catholic School, Santiago, Chile

IRISH REPUBLIC, NORTHERN IRELAND, WALES, SCOTLAND CHAPTER 17
Sharon Hancock, TV Reporter, Dublin
Miss McAffee, Grade School Teacher, Belfast

Derek Law, School Principal, Llandrindod, Wales
Ogilvy and Mather, Edinburgh

Norway Chapter 18
Alla and Rafael Golden, Oslo
Oslo Children's Museum
Gordon Kallio, Ogilvy and Mather, San Francisco
Ogilvy and Mather, Oslo
Garth Uibel, High School Teacher, Indio, California
Gro Harlem Brundtland, Prime Minster of Norway
Ambassador and Mrs. Robert Stuart, U.S. Embassy, Oslo
Angel Tourism, Turkish travel agency

New Zealand and Australia Chapter 19
New Zealand Rotary Club
Mary Robbins, Ogilvy and Mather, San Francisco
U.S. Consulate, Auckland
Rotary Club, Sidney
"Today Show," Sidney

Papua New Guinea Chapter 20
U.S. Congressman Tom Lantos, San Mateo, California
U.S. Embassy, Port Moresby
San Francisco Day School, San Francisco

Yugoslavia, Turkey, Greece Chapter 21
St. Catherine's School, Burlingame, California
Franciscan Monks, Yugoslavia
Garth Uibel, Indio High School Teacher, Indio, California
School Principal, Ankara, Turkey

Saudi Arabia Chapter 22
St. Catherine's School, Burlingame, California
Mr. Awaken, U.S. Expediter, Jedda
Jay and Maria Frerres, Consul General and Wife, Jedda
Mobil Oil, Jedda

San Francisco Chapter 24
Audrey Hepburn, UNICEF, San Francisco

Rome Chapter 25
Elizabeth and Gerry Beaulaurier, San Mateo, California
Father Miles Riley, San Francisco Archdiocese
Monsignor Steven Otellini, San Francisco

Smithsonian Institution
Suzanne Orcutt, First Director of Paintbrush Diplomacy
Sheri Sobrato, President, Board of Directors, San Francisco Peninsula

VOLUNTEERS FOR
PAINTBRUSH DIPLOMACY

Lois Behnke
Pat Keefe
George Kristovich
Norma Kristovich
Annette Legallet
Laura Lemaire
Barbara Levinson
Art Moskin
Mel Pincus
Lee Quinley
John Ranahan
Ron Rosenberg
Joe Thorn
Others too numerous to mention.

Special appreciation to Tom and Annette Lantos for donating their collection of children's paintings to Paintbrush Diplomacy in 1999.

We thank all of you and the children for painting our world a little brighter!

Char and Rudy

A FEW FACTS ABOUT PAINTBRUSH DIPLOMACY FOR THE YEAR 2000

People reached through our members' mailing lists	4,000
People our press materials reach	1.2 million
Teachers who participate in our program each year	600
Gallery visitors each month	1,000
Hits on our Web site each month	500
Children served by our educational programs each year	18,500
Visitors to traveling exhibits each year	25,000

COUNTRIES PARTICIPATING IN PAINTBRUSH DIPLOMACY TO THE YEAR 2000

Albania	Germany	Norway
Argentina	Greece	Oman
Australia	Guatemala	Panama
Austria	Guyana	Papua New Guinea
Bahamas	Haiti	Peru
Bahrain	Honduras	Philippines
Bangladesh	Hong Kong	Poland
Belgium	Hungary	Portugal
Bermuda	Iceland	Qatar
Bhutan	India	Romania
Bolivia	Indonesia	Saudi Arabia
Botswana	Iran	Scotland
Bulgaria	Iraq	Singapore
Brazil	Ireland	South Africa
Burkina Faso	Israel	Spain
Cameroon	Italy	Sri Lanka
Canada	Ivory Coast	Sweden
Cent. African Rep.	Jamaica	Switzerland
Chile	Japan	Syria
China	Kenya	Taiwan
Colombia	Korea	Thailand
Congo (Zaire)	Kuwait	Tunisia
Croatia	Latvia	Turkey
Czech Rep.	Lesotho	Uganda
Cyprus	Lithuania	Ukraine
Denmark	Malawi	United Arab Emirates
Dominican Rep.	Malaysia	Uruguay
Ecuador	Mexico	USA
Egypt	Morocco	Venezuela
England	Myanmar	Vietnam
Estonia	Nepal	Wales
Fiji	New Zealand	Yugoslavia
Finland	Netherlands	Zimbabwe
France	Nigeria	

Colophon

This book represents the heartfelt work of many devoted individuals. Designed by Barbara Lande, with production assistance from Natalie Harwood, who patiently scanned the children's art for reproduction and gracefully handled many details. The front cover illustration is by the author, Char Pribuss. The back cover illustration was created by Jeremiah S. Gaela, when he was 11 years old.

The text face is ITC Berkeley, originally designed for the University of California Press in Berkeley by Frederic W. Goudy in 1938. This version was a redrawing by Tony Stan. The san serif font is Myria, designed by Carol Twombly and Robert Slimbach.

The book was printed at California Lithographers, Concord, California.